*To my dear fr[iend] ~~Tim and Chris~~,
Here's another fast read you[ ] ght
enjoy. Hugs to both, + particularly
your son,
Harry Gossett*

FOREWARNED

By
Harry Gossett

Copyright © 2014 Harry Gossett
All rights reserved.

ISBN: 1503225062
ISBN 13: 9781503225060
Library of Congress Control Number: 2014920974
CreateSpace Independent Publishing Platform
North Charleston, South Carolina

DISCLAIMERS

A prepublication review of this novella was conducted by the Federal Bureau of Investigation (FBI) because the author is a twenty-year veteran of the FBI.

The publication approval letter requested:
"... please incorporate a disclaimer advising readers that the opinions expressed in the novella are yours and not those of the FBI."

Please be so advised.

This is a work of fiction. Any resemblance to actual persons, living or dead, events, or locales is entirely coincidental.

ACKNOWLEDGMENTS

This little book would have been far less readable without generous contributions of time and expertise by two great guys:

James Grady, author of ***LAST DAYS OF THE CONDOR*** and many other wonderful novels.

Wayne Barnes, author of an intriguing, soon-to-be-published spy novel, from an insider's point of view.

CHAPTER ONE

The Urban Nomad

• • •

What an exquisite moment, his dream coming true—her fluffy hair tickling his face, her warm breath on his neck, her panting in his ear—he moaned with pleasure without opening his eyes.

Quivering with excitement, eager for his touch, she stuck her hot, wet tongue in his ear and jolted him wide awake.

He grabbed her abundant hair with both hands and gently pushed her back.

"Ginger! It's you!"

The Afghan hound licked her chops, happy to be spoken to, hopped down off the couch and watched the forty-four-year-old man stretch his muscular frame.

"I forgot where I was," Lance told her as he hoisted all six feet of himself to his feet.

She sat down and panted, focused on his blue eyes, which always looked like he was expecting to learn something, and disguising his habitual skepticism.

"Yeah, I know, I'm the guy who never forgets anything—except what it's like to be kissed awake." He sighed. "What a deal."

He had Ginger's undivided attention.

"Did Ralph feed you already?"

She gave him a big doggy smile.

He crossed the room and took his toothbrush and razor out of his suit jacket, crumpled with his pants in the overstuffed chair, not a shabby suit, merely treated that way.

"Look at my suit," he continued his happy chat with Ginger. "Did you sleep on my suit? Yes, you did." Lance could mimic any accent, but baby talk was the best he could do with a dog.

His package of fresh laundry was still wrapped in paper.

"At least you didn't unwrap my shirt and shorts. No, you didn't," he said, shaking his head, nose to nose with the waist-high hound, "so all of me won't have to smell like you today."

When Lance turned away, Ginger tagged along with him to the bathroom, starved for company in her little world of Ralph's one-bedroom apartment.

Just as though she could understand, or would care, Lance told her, "Ralph said I could use some of his toothpaste. Yes, he did. And some of his shaving cream, too."

After Lance brushed his teeth he noticed a few gray hairs among his whiskers. "Bad enough I'm getting gray around the edges," he told Ginger, "but someday soon I'm going to have a salt-and-pepper five-o'clock shadow."

A shower after his shave, then he got into his clean underwear and fresh shirt and felt ready to face the day—fresh breath, clean shaven, odor free. Unfortunately, he still had to wear the suit that smelled of *eau de Ginger.*

The life of a metropolitan drifter may sound romantic, but while normal folks walk barefoot from room to room to get dressed, transients like Lance Walker have to trudge from building to building. On this particular day in the spring of 1994, it was all the way across town.

Walking is often the fastest way to get around the island of Manhattan because you can never find a place to park a car; you don't need much space to park your feet, but you'd better wear thick socks and comfortable shoes. Lance wore rubber-soled oxfords which allowed him to glide silently, a basic necessity for a New York City private investigator and the reason they are often referred to as "gumshoes."

He strolled across the Sheep Meadow in Central Park, where no sheep had grazed since the 1930s when they were removed so homeless people couldn't eat them. Traffic sounds were muffled by the trees, and the air smelled of clover. Lance knew from personal experience, two-thirds of his lifetime ago, that the meadow would be carpeted with students from expensive private high schools sitting with their cliques in the spring grass at lunchtime. But midmorning on this particular day, all Lance saw were lovers strolling hand-in-hand.

He thought: *Too bad they don't allow dogs on the Sheep Meadow; Ginger could get a good run here every day and not have to wait for Ralph to take her to the country on weekends.*

Dark clouds threatened rain. In the manmade meadow it was easy to forget he was in the middle of the most densely populated city in the United States.

With his dirty shirt, smelly socks, and soiled underwear folded in the laundry paper that, earlier, had been wrapped around their clean replacements, he took the homemade package back to the same Chinese laundry on the West Side.

As usual, there was a new Chinese guy behind the counter.

They probably just pass through here on their way from China to somewhere else in the USA.

"You pick this up last night?" the Asian man asked with a heavy accent and a puzzled look.

"No," said Lance. He pointed to the shirt he was wearing. "I picked *this* up last night."

The counter man nodded and filled out a ticket, which went into Lance's side pocket, crinkled together with two similar reminders of places he had, also, left clothes.

"Fold for drawer?" asked the eager Asian.

Lance had to laugh. "You *are* my drawer."

While non-nomads scarfed down their breakfasts in the relative comfort of their own homes, Lance missed his as he walked to the dry cleaners, just three short blocks north, to finish dressing.

Since 1811 the avenues in Manhattan have run north and south, about twenty blocks to the mile, with commercial establishments on the ground floors of nearly all the buildings, some emitting enticing food smells.

I should have stopped for breakfast at one of the two coffee shops I passed, or at least picked up a piece of fruit from the Korean fruit stand.

CHAPTER TWO

The Whistle Blower

• • •

In the dry cleaners, the young man talking to the owner at the far end of the counter didn't draw Lance's attention away from the fetching female, who was fetching his clean suit off the rack.

She said, "Here you are, Mr. Walker."

At the sound of the name "Walker," the man's head snapped around and his horn-rimmed glasses almost fell off his face. He adjusted his thick spectacles and studied Lance Walker. The lad wore an ill-fitting, plaid suit, a clip-on tie, and tacky loafers. He shuffled papers in a cheap briefcase on the counter in front of him.

Lance pretended he didn't notice the younger man's agitated attention.

"Someplace to change?" Lance asked the pretty clerk.

"Fitting Room. Right over there," she said with a smile that made her even more attractive.

While Lance changed into his fresh suit and tie, he wondered how the guy with the cheap briefcase knew his name, and why it excited him.

When Lance came out of the fitting room, the lad was gone.

The comely clerk took the suit and tie that smelled of Ginger. She gave Lance another ticket and another pleasing smile.

Outside, Lance ran right into the chap with the shoddy shoes and plaid suit.

"Mr. Walker?"

Lance eyed him from top to bottom, and back up to top.

The anxious young man held his bargain-basement briefcase in front of his chest like a shield. He seemed terrified. He swallowed hard and repeated, "Lance Walker?"

Lance nodded, cautiously.

What the hell, he knows my full name.

The younger man looked all around, and then gestured for Lance to follow him into one of the few alleys in Manhattan.

As nervous as he is, I know this geek is no hitman.

In the filthy alley, the nerd looked around again before he said, "Mr. Walker, I'm with the Internal Revenue Service, and I've got something for you."

A tidal wave of depression drenched Lance Walker. His past had caught up with him—again.

What a kick in the crotch!

The acid in Lance's empty stomach burbled. He asked, "A summons for all my books and records?"

I should have denied I'm Lance Walker!

The tax man shook his head and checked over his shoulder.

Why the hell is HE so agitated?

"Not another search warrant for my person," said Lance. "I thought you guys had given up on that crap after the tax court ---"

"No." The Revenue Officer shifted around like a man who has to pee real bad.

Lance's head swirled. "I thought when we elected Bill Clinton president he'd sic you guys on the big-time tax cheats and leave us little guys alone."

"I wouldn't know about that."

The dry cleaner's ticket crackled in Lance's shaking hand. "You already know where my other suit is. You might want to wait a couple of days and seize it after it's been cleaned."

The young man said, "I'm not going to seize anything."

A horn honked nearby and gave the lad a start. He recovered and said, "I just think it's a crime how the Service is wasting its resources on a guy like you."

"Yeah," said Lance, "I'm the only guy who ever went to jail for paying his taxes."

"Jail?"

"I guess you're too young to remember. I got a month in the can for *Contempt Of Court*."

"Just because you wouldn't identify your clients?"

"Still won't, so you're wasting your time."

The bureaucrat fidgeted around some more, nervous as a new prisoner in the shower. "But you do pay your taxes?"

"Sure. But I don't keep any documents. You guys have a habit of seizing them."

Fortunately, the IRS wonk didn't ask him how he kept track of his income without written records. He never would have believed that Lance does it all in his head. It's not as hard as it sounds.

Stepping in close, the taxman lowered his voice to a conspiratorial whisper. "Look, there's an asshole named Whittaker, a Branch Manager in Texas till he did something awful down there, got busted to Group Supervisor, and transferred to New York."

"Uh-huh."

The kid checked all around again, and moved in even closer. "Whittaker wants to redeem himself. Since nobody else has been able to nail you, he figures if he can ---"

"God knows they've tried." As soon as Lance interrupted, he realized he had cut off a man trying to tell him something he shouldn't, so Lance shut up and let the kid talk.

The government agent looked all around again, and even up at the windows above the alley, before he went on. "No one knows where you sleep."

Hell, half the time I don't know where I'm going to sleep.

"Whittaker can't find you to start surveillance so he posted an administrative bounty for any IRS employee who spots you and calls it in to him."

Oh no! I'm in the tax-crap up to my assets, again.

Lance said, "That's a swell use of the taxpayers' money."

His new best friend shrugged and continued his nervous dance.

It isn't this guy's fault.

FOREWARNED

Lance pointed to a public telephone and said, "There's a phone on the corner."

One of those aggressive New York pigeons flapped by the tense tax man's face. He nearly jumped out of his rumpled suit, then took a deep, ragged breath and said, "Any IRS employee who sees you and calls it in to Whittaker, in time for him to lock onto you, gets a free Administrative Leave day. He even posted your picture on the bulletin board."

Nice of taxboy to warn me.

Taxboy looked over his shoulder for the thirty-fifth time. "There are over three thousand of us on the streets in Manhattan."

3,000 tax collectors on a 22-square-mile island equals over 136 feds per square mile looking for me! The prospect of a day off in the suburbs of New Jersey, or Long Island, or wherever the hell they

17

live, is all the inducement they need to memorize my arrest picture and keep their eyes open all day, every day. One of those dorks is bound to see me and collect the bounty anyway, so it might as well be this kid with a conscience.

"Want to make the call now and collect an extra day off?" asked Lance.

"I've never seen you, sir." He was breathing hard.

"And I've never seen you, but if you want a day off, I'd understand."

The young man shook his head. "Thanks anyway. We've got an office pool with $1,400 in it. I bet that you'd last till tomorrow night." He scurried away.

To give the whistleblower time to distance himself, Lance paced and pondered in the stinking alley for five minutes, and then skulked down a one-way street against the traffic.

CHAPTER THREE

Doing The Math

• • •

The numbered streets in Manhattan run east and west, about ten blocks to the mile. The majority of them are one-way, in alternating directions, lined with boutique businesses and apartments in big old brownstone residences which were built for large families with servants in an era when the affluent had large families and servants.

Lance stopped at a payphone where he automatically thought: My taxable income is $18,722.67.

He wiped the earpiece off with his handkerchief and dropped a quarter in the phone to make a business call. The phone *bonged.*

Now my taxable income is $18,722.42. How simple it is to keep track, and I don't even round off to the nearest dollar like the IRS.

Eighteen-thousand dollars might not sound like much money to live on in New York City in 1994, but Lance didn't pay rent, many of his meals were free, and it was still early in the year.

He yawned and stretched to discretely check behind him for watchers while he waited for Janet to answer.

Her pleasant voice came on the line, "Good morning. May I help you?"

To avoid telephone taps by the minions of the Infernal Residue Service, Lance's sister kept his telephone in her law office, listed to her.

"Today is the twenty-fifth," said he. It was their secret code.

"Oh crap, are we going to have to do that again?" It was bad enough that she had to act as his message service.

"Yeah, there's a new IRS hotshot on my case."

"They won't bug my phone," she said. "No court would allow it."

She was right. It's tough to get a court to authorize a tap on a lawyer's telephone—lawyer-client privilege, if not professional courtesy.

"So they won't ask a court. It was my number before it became your private line."

Lance heard the sound of paper being shuffled: his message slips.

"There's a Mr. Barkley—" she said, as she started to add the number 25 to the last two digits of the telephone number, with a pencil.

"Now that's a blast from the past. I haven't heard from him in about ten years. His number still ends in 8756?" Lance had already done the addition in his head.

"Hold on," said Janet, "I'm a lawyer, not a mathematician." When she reached the same total, she said, "Your memory never ceases to amaze me."

She was such a brilliant over-achiever that besting her at anything was a joy for her younger brother. He could only outdo her in math and memory.

"Good memory ought to be hereditary," said Lance.

His sister chuckled, "Whatever memory genes our parents had, you got."

He moved her along with the word fragment "'kay," a New York abbreviation for the word "Okay."

She shuffled paper and said, "Then there's a Mr. Lee ---"

"'kay."

She added, "He said it is most urgent he see you as soon as possible."

"'kay."

Another shuffle, then Janet said, "Mrs. Karris called to remind you you're having dinner with her tonight."

How could a guy forget that?

"'kay."

Janet wanted to know about Mrs. Karris, but didn't want to ask. She said, "I told her you haven't forgotten anything as long as I've known you -- and that's all my life. She said you can sleep over."

No wonder Janet is curious.

"'kay."

Janet paused and waited, until she realized he wasn't going to tell her about Mrs. Karris. Then she said, "And that's it."

"'kay. Talk to you later."

Janet dropped the message slips in her shredder. Maybe it's not called a shredder. It chops the paper into confetti, so perhaps it should be called a chipper. Lance had bought it for her after he reassembled a shredded document for a client. It took two days, but if the paper had been chipped into little diamonds it couldn't have been put back together at all.

CHAPTER FOUR

Through The Trees To Mr. Lee's

• • •

No breakfast for Lance today. He had to hurry back across Central Park to Mr. Lee's house, or rather, Mr. Lee's *mansion*.

When Frederick Law Olmsted designed Central Park in the 1850s, he said he wanted every turn to offer a brand new vista. His *Greensward Plan* for the park provided perfect surveillance detection routes for paranoid pedestrians like Lance Walker had just become. He had to dodge between joggers on West Drive, but far fewer of them than he would have encountered earlier in the morning, and he knew IRS agents wouldn't be running around the park in shorts while on duty.

Despite his rush, Lance stopped in a pedestrian tunnel to make sure no one was following him. As he watched, he listened to the bass drone of a didgeridoo played by a Nordic blonde boy crouched behind the big wooden tube. With only his breath, the aboriginal Australian instrument vibrated the big gray stone blocks fitted snugly into this two-hundred-foot long arch, there for more than a century. Lance and the musician, with his bulging eyes, were alone in the passageway for several minutes. Finally, the woodwind player stopped and said, "Doesn't it sound awesome in here?" Lance smiled, nodded, and, released from the mesmerizing sound, took his leave.

A few more trails between boulders, around a fountain, beside the shallow sailboat lake, and through the trees of Central Park, gave Lance many opportunities to discretely check his back trail. He detected no IRS folks following him, but the effort reminded him of how he got onto their hit-list in the first place.

Years before, they found out that his bank deposits were made in cash, so they decided he fit the profile of a money-launderer. They were wrong, of course. The cash deposits were made to protect his clients' identities, even in his own bank records. He cashed client checks at their own banks and then deposited the money in his account in his bank. He didn't evade any taxes.

The IRS wouldn't believe him because he wouldn't tell them who his clients were, so they could verify his story. They seized all of his files, and they were disappointed. They found nothing but a few expense records. He kept information in his head and reported it, orally, to his clients, none of whom were crooks, but all of whom preferred that the folks they had him investigate not find out about it.

The net result was the IRS made Lance Walker a homeless person through jeopardy assessments and seizures of his property. They seized his bank accounts as the proceeds of crime, levied income taxes on those funds, and then seized all his assets so he couldn't convert them to cash and flee the country, which, of course, he had no desire to do. He no longer had an office, a car, a private investigator's license, a pistol permit, a listed telephone, or a fixed address, but the IRS still wasn't through with him. They suspected he had laundered money for felons, and they wouldn't give up until he identified the sources of his income.

But the notoriety of his case enhanced his business. It also inspired a draconian judge to reconsider his own proclamation. The judge had promised Lance he would stay in the Federal Correctional Center until he decided to talk, but then let him go after his case became a lightning rod for all sorts of anti-IRS protesters who picketed the courthouse.

One name Lance refused to divulge was Mr. Lee.

Mr. Lee's home was built a century ago by a railroad tycoon who had just returned from a long vacation in France, so he constructed a French chateau in the middle of Manhattan. The mogul had other mansions, some more palatial than this one, which were sprinkled around the circuit of fashionable places in the world.

A liveried butler showed Lance into Mr. Lee's home office, a well-appointed room with mahogany walls and matching bookshelves between wide, floor-to-ceiling windows. The room felt cold and had no apparent aroma. The natty client sat behind a huge French writing-table.

The butler announced the obvious, "Mr. Lee, Mr. Walker is here."

Mr. Lee waited calmly until the butler withdrew, then abruptly stood up, rushed around the table, and said, "Walker, I'm grateful you came so quickly!" He pumped Lance's hand.

"Your message said it was 'most urgent.'"

"It's my granddaughter, Jennifer," said the old man, "She's run away from home."

Mr. Lee's anxiety was obvious.

"How old is she?" asked Lance.

"Fifteen."

No wonder he's worried. The onset of estrogen is a dangerous time.

"That's not good," said Lance.

"It's worse than that. She telephoned her mother to say she's never coming back."

Lance grimaced.

"They have Caller ID on their telephone," said Mr. Lee.

"Where did she call from?"

"The number turns out to be a public phone on Times Square."

"She could have just been passing through. The Port Authority Bus Station is located ---"

"No, Jennifer told my daughter-in-law she had found a place, and that she was 'staying right here.'" Mr. Lee made quote marks in the air with his fingers.

Lance had never seen him upset before.

"That's doesn't sound good."

"I gave a picture of Jennifer to the police Runaway Squad, but they haven't been able to find her."

So much for my first suggestion.

"Have another copy of her picture?"

"Of course." Mr. Lee plucked a photograph from his inside pocket and handed it to Lance.

Jennifer Lee is one luscious little lady. That only makes my task more critical.

So far as Times Square prostitution was concerned, every night was amateur night, not to mention drugs, alcohol, physical violence, emotional abuse, incurable diseases, some of which hadn't even been named yet, and every other disaster that can happen to a delicate girl from the upscale exurbs.

Mr. Lee's face was one big question mark. His anxious breathing whistled through his nose.

"I'll try," said Lance.

Mr. Lee looked relieved and said, "If you take her home, she will simply run away again, so please bring her here."

Like so many rats, a thousand facts Lance knew from experience gnawed away at Mr. Lee's notion that he could pull this tiny white rabbit out of that huge grubby hat.

His confidence in my ability is far greater than my own.

Lance said, "If I can get her to call you, can you convince her to live here?"

"I'll give her anything she wants, if you can just get her off the street."

Mr. Lee leaned in close and said, "And I'll give *you* anything you want if you can do it." He was serious.

"Hell, I've been charging limousine rides to your account for years."

"You don't use my limo account nearly enough, Mr. Walker, just a couple of times a month."

It would have been better for Lance if Mr. Lee had an account with a cab company or with a car service that didn't use stretch limousines. But now was not the time to complain, or to explain

FOREWARNED

why he so seldom used Mr. Lee's regal mode of transport.

Mr. Lee said, "And you went to jail rather than give the government my name!"

"You wouldn't have been in any trouble if I *had* given them your name. I just check out potential investors for you. Seems to me that steering clear of dirty money is every honest investment banker's duty."

Mr. Lee shook his head. "If my clients had found out I had them investigated, it would have ruined me." He opened the center drawer in the French writing-table. It was filled with banded stacks of twenty-dollar bills. "I'm prepared to pay whatever it costs ---"

"Just be prepared to pay attention—to Jennifer—if I can get her to call you."

Mr. Lee picked up two packets of cash. *$5,000.00* was printed on the paper bands wrapped around each of them. "You may need ready cash for necessary operating expenses."

Lance took one of the packets, dropped it in his pocket, and said, "Times Square can be an expensive neighborhood."

$5,000.00 added to $18,722.42 gives me $23,722.42 net income.

CHAPTER FIVE

A Chip Off The Old Barkley

• • •

Outside the Lee mansion, Lance looked around. No IRS mopes were lurking on the quiet street, at least none were visible.

Lance glided through the opulent neighborhood, stone-faced buildings with stone-faced doormen, poseurs in expensive clothes walking expensive dogs, which were doing exactly the same thing the inexpensive dogs do.

At Fifth Avenue, Lance boarded a downtown bus and swayed along with the other standing passengers as they lurched through the traffic.

The $1.50 bus fare subtracted from $23,722.42 leaves $23,720.92 as my up-to-the-minute, net taxable income.

See. It's simple. Well, it was simple for Lance Walker.

It was still too early in the day to expect a runaway teenage girl to be out and about, so Lance had time to visit his old client, Hal Barkley, on his way to Times Square.

Barkley's law office was in a glass and chrome, midtown skyscraper right across Fifth Avenue from a bus stop. Lance used the reflections in the glass front at ground level to see if anyone was on his tail. He didn't see anyone who looked like an IRS agent.

In the posh reception room on the twenty-third floor he met a very businesslike, well-coiffed receptionist, who smelled of lilac and spoke with a British accent, "May I be of assistance, sir?"

Lance said, "I'm here to see Hal Barkley."

"You're too late," she said. "Mr. Barkley died three years ago."

"But ... but ... he just called me this morning, from Hal Barkley's number."

"If a Mr. Barkley called you from here this morning," she said, officiously, "it must have been Hal Barkley's son, Norman Barkley. Whom shall I say is calling?"

Norman Barkley didn't look much like his dad, but he occupied Hal's huge oak-paneled office and studied Lance from behind his father's big oaken desk.

"My father had a great deal of confidence in you, Mr. Walker," said the short, skinny Ivy Leaguer. "He told me you went to jail for contempt rather than identify your clients."

"That, unfortunately, is my claim to fame." Lance sat down, uninvited.

"Frankly, I've always found that the scope of our information needs in corporate litigation requires the depth one can only secure from a much larger investigative organization than yours."

That wouldn't require much depth. With me, what you see is what you get.

Lance suggested, "But now you've found a case small enough for me to work on?"

"No. It's a case of potentially leviathan proportions, with numerous collateral pitfalls. We have already engaged eleven different private inquiry agencies in nine countries ---"

"Who haven't found out what you need to know."

"That's correct."

Lance always enjoyed being hired by a client who has been *big-firmed*. That experience made whatever he was able to learn look great, and whatever he charged look small.

Barkley-the-Younger resumed, "I've decided to give you a chance to impress me as favorably as you did my father."

What a piece of work this kid is.

"I'm no longer a licensed private investigator," said Lance.

"Oh. What do you do now?"

"I call it *research*."

"We have a dozen researchers on staff."

"I could be your *outside* researcher."

"Okay," said Lawyer Barkley.

"Research regarding …?"

"Well, my client, Randolph Drysdale, owned and operated Drysdale Package Service, until Westwood Express purchased Drysdale Package Service in order to enter the European market. Mr. Drysdale managed the European operations under his sales contract with Westwood Express, but his philosophy conflicted with Dan Tyler's. He's the Chief Executive Officer of Westwood."

"I know who Dan Tyler is."

The snide lawyer said, "You'd have to be comatose not to." Then he continued. "Finally, Mr. Drysdale resigned. Pursuant to the sales agreement, Mr. Drysdale waited three years to re-enter the industry. He then started Common Market Delivery, which has beaten Westwood Express in the European marketplace ever since."

"I see," said Lance.

"Last year, someone reported to the Drug Enforcement Administration that Common Market Delivery knowingly transports narcotics for drug cartels."

Ah ha! Now we get to the nitty and the gritty.

Lance said, "The DEA gets all kinds of nut calls."

"The DEA investigated and is satisfied that the report is unfounded, but they won't tell Mr. Drysdale the source of the allegation," said Barkley. "News articles have popped up in European papers reporting that the DEA is investigating Common Market Delivery. Suits have been filed against the newspapers, but they refuse to divulge their sources."

The oldest trick in the book: Report some crap to the authorities, then plant the story that they are investigating. Inside sources at the law enforcement agency confirm to the press that the allegation is in the files, and the news media destroys your target's reputation for you, while you remain anonymous.

"You think Tyler is behind it?" asked Lance.

"We're sure Tyler is behind it," said Barkley. "We're threatening to sue, but we don't have a scrap of proof—yet."

"Despite engaging eleven different private inquiry agencies, each with great depth, in nine countries?"

Lance couldn't resist razzing him a little. He even thought about asking how many continents, but thought better of it.

Barkley ignored the jibe and went on, "Tyler denies all knowledge. He enjoys the public image of a clean-cut, American boy who made good. His lawyers are threatening to sue us, as well as Mr. Drysdale, if we so much as suggest that Mr. Tyler had anything to do with spreading a malicious lie."

Where to start?

"Could I have a list of the reporters and papers that covered the story?"

The lawyer patted a stack of newspapers on his desk. "I have copies for you here."

Lawyers love pieces of papers. Lance didn't.

"No thanks." Lance put his hands in his pockets. "Just let me read the names of the newspapers and the names of the journalists."

Barkley turned the newspapers around so Lance could read them.

Lance didn't tell his client that he prefers to read upside down. It keeps him in practice to scan the stuff on people's desks and read the notes they are taking without arousing suspicion.

The top newspaper was *The London Leader* and it had the headline: DRYSDALE DISPATCHES DOPE, above an article by Michael Slyker.

This looks like the work of Connally; planting disinformation is his specialty.

Lance said, "Whoever gave Michael Slyker this information first made the report to the DEA."

"Even *we* figured that out." Barkley's tone was condescending.

I can hardly negotiate a fee while he is in this frame of mind.

The exciting thing about conducting investigations is you don't know what you are going to find out, until you find it out. However, in some cases, all you can find out is that you can't find out anything.

Lance still hadn't had his breakfast, but he now had the IRS to worry about. He had accepted two cases with "dismal disappointment" written all over them. It wasn't shaping up to be a great day.

Lance exited Barkley's building on the ramp from the underground-parking garage that opened at ground level on the side street, just in case IRS agents had the lobby covered. They were on his mind, but not in his view, as he moved through the rivers of pedestrians in the manmade canyons created by tall buildings towering above miniscule earthlings, scurrying about on the sidewalks of Manhattan.

The reflection in the glass on the side of the bus shelter made a good mirror to check for the IRS while Lance waited for the cross-town bus. A full-color poster advertised *Pinky's Clip Joint*, a hairdressing establishment. The ad featured the smiling face of a middle-aged man. Beneath it were the words: *My mother dyed twenty years before I was born.*

CHAPTER SIX

The Worst Of Times Square

• • •

Lance reached Times Square in time for the lunch rush and deducted $1.50 bus fare from his taxable income of $23,720.92 and got $23,719.42. Had he thought to get one in advance, a cross-town bus transfer would have been free.

Times Square isn't square. Formed by Broadway and Seventh Avenue cutting diagonally across one another, it's shaped like the last two slices of stale pizza pointing at each other from opposite sides of the box. This box is bordered by Fortieth Street, Eighth Avenue, Fifty-third Street, and Sixth Avenue—six million square feet which encompasses the Theatre District.

Despite the city's efforts to tidy it up, Times Square looked a lot cleaner on television than it did on the ground; the sidewalks were sticky. Lance saw more grime than glitz. Wide-eyed tourists and street-wise hustlers obstructed the passage of dashing commuters who herded toward the Port Authority Bus Terminal. Throngs of bargain hunters frequented fast-food stands and fly-by-night stores, which sold discount (often stolen or knock-off) electronic equipment, cameras, jewelry, and assorted junk. These establishments shared ground-level storefronts with porn shops, peep shows, strip joints and sleazy bars. Human body odor hung in the air, and the cacophony of traffic was everywhere. The neighborhood was particularly depressing on an overcast day.

The best place to hide is in a crowd, but Lance had conducted enough surveillance to know a crowd hides the hunter as well as the hunted. For the first time, he was both. Just as the lunchtime crowd in Times Square would make it difficult for IRS employees to spot him, it would make it equally difficult for him to see them, particularly if they saw him first.

Times Square is dangerous territory. As a group, IRS types have shown more interest in the seamier side of life than other investigators. So there's probably a greater concentration of them here in Times Square.

As he trolled the area, he divided his attention among the bozos, who looked like they might be IRS employees, Jennifer Lee's photograph, and the faces of teenage hookers working the streets. Over street noises he could hear the little darlings, in their revealing outfits, hitting on every male passerby.

"Excuse me, can you light my cigarette?" and "Looking for a date?" and "Want to party?"

Guys are suckers for teenage girls and willing women, and these kids were both. They looked around furtively for their pimps and police, then threw themselves at total strangers who had to have something seriously wrong with them to desire a tryst in this cesspool.

Lance bought a coke and a dirty-water hot dog with blood-red onions from a street vendor.

Wonder what germs I'm subjecting myself to? Helluva a brunch!

A couple of hours at Times Square, without a glimpse of the elusive Ms. Lee, or any IRS agents following him, proved to be all Lance could stand.

The sky still looked like steel wool, threatening to rain all day long.

FOREWARNED

A good rain would have been good for me. It would have washed away a lot of dirt, driven most of these people off the streets, stripped away the human cover, and exposed the amateur hookers and IRS lookers.

CHAPTER SEVEN

The Media Magician

• • •

Thoughts of rain kept reminding Lance he needed to pee. There was a dearth of public restrooms in Manhattan in 1994. Bars and restaurants put *Out-of-Order* signs on bathroom doors so they could reject the piss trade. Lance plodded his way to a private club in a marble mansion just a few blocks to the east, geographically, but worlds away, culturally.

The mix of establishments was eclectic. The New York City Bar Association building was bracketed by bars. A church stood next to an S&M club, brokerage firms, travel agencies, and all sorts of stores and spas were jumbled together. There were lots of potential IRS employees doing their jobs there.

You never realize how many nerdy people wander around the streets of New York until you start looking for them.

The International Club occupied a marble-front building specifically constructed for it at the end of the nineteenth century. Membership was considered only for those sponsored by current members, and who would also pay $25,000 per year for the privilege of eating less than remarkable food in a quiet retreat in the heart of the hectic city.

The uniformed doorman stopped Lance. "Sorry, sir, only members and their guests are allowed."

"Obviously, you're new here," said Lance in the haughty tone such servants have come to expect from their arrogant patrons.

"I've been here twelve years," said the doorman, apologetically.

"Then you *should* be sorry." Lance marched right past him.

The doorman hurriedly reviewed the list of members.

I wonder what he's looking for. I didn't give him my name.

Lance had the advantage. Having once lunched in this club, he sort of knew his way around. Since he didn't want to be announced, he cut through the bar and slipped up the back stairs to the second floor dining room, just in case the doorman recovered his nerve and sent someone after him. Unfortunately, Lance didn't know where to find a men's room, on route. But he knew his quarry would be in the third floor reading room, if he wasn't out ruining someone's reputation, so Lance used another flight of creaky stairs, rather than the antique elevator.

The sinister old info-provocateur sat in an overstuffed leather chair reading a newspaper in a musty room full of old men in overstuffed leather chairs reading newspapers. He sat apart from the others. Lance wondered if that was his choice or theirs. As he glided over to him, Lance noticed a stack of foreign newspapers beside his chair.

No doubt, he's reviewing the results of his skullduggery.

Before Connally noticed, Lance sat down right across from him.

The old man looked up over his half-moon glasses and said, "How did you get in here?"

"Someone mounted a disinformation operation against a client of mine," said Lance. "It reminded me of you."

Connally chuckled. "Managing the news is no crime, Walker. Who's your client?"

"Drysdale."

Connally chuckled again. "I wouldn't tell you if I was involved." He dropped his voice to a whisper. "An insignificant independent like you could get killed in a hell of a hurry."

Lance whispered back, "You threatening me?"

Connally looked around. "Just a word to the wise."

"If an insignificant independent like me gets threatened by a guy like you, who could deliver on a death threat ..." Lance closed in, eyeball-to-eyeball, smelled the Cuban cigars on Connally's breath, and returned the warning, "I would be a fool to wait around for you to try. The only reasonable reaction would be to eliminate the threat as quickly as possible."

Connally didn't flinch. He even raised the stakes. "I'll never warn you again."

Lance didn't blink either. "Nor I, you."

Lance rose to leave, knowing he had worse than wasted his time here.

The old villain didn't given me any helpful hints, and now he knows I'm on the case. He might decide to have me killed. Connally's the sort of man who could arrange a murder.

Inexplicably, Lance didn't feel the need to pee so urgently anymore.

The doorman tried to challenge him again on his way out, but Lance ignored him. He identified two IRS guys across the street who had recognized their ticket to a free day off. They stumbled around and bumped into each other, unsure what they should do with their lucky break.

Too bad the nice one I met this morning didn't make the call. Now he won't get a day off, nor win his bet that I would elude them for another twenty-four hours.

CHAPTER EIGHT

Walking The Bloodhounds

• • •

The two lucky vacation-day winners followed Lance to Madison Avenue where he held up his left wrist and pretended to check his watch. (He never wore a watch.) He bought a paper at a newsstand, unfolded it, and refolded it lengthwise, like New Yorkers do when they read the newspaper on a crowded subway. It didn't catch the wind that way, and he could see around it while pretending to scan the articles. Despite his upside-down reading preference, he held it right-side-up to look like a normal reader.

In the rearview mirror on a parked car, Lance watched the tax collectors make the all-important telephone call from a public phone.

Deduct the twenty-five cents for the newspaper from my taxable income of $23,719.42 and get $23,719.17. The newspaper is a legitimate deduction. It helps me protect my sources of income from unwanted scrutiny that would dry them up. I wouldn't have purchased the paper if I didn't need it as a professional prop.

Lance put one of his soft-rubber shoe soles up on top of a fire hydrant and read the newspaper. If he had to stand for an extended period of time, he usually put a foot up on something. It eased his lower backache. The streets of New York can be painfully hard after a few minutes of standing still, even in cushioned shoes.

Lance waited for his new nemesis to arrive.

Once I get a look at Mr. Whittaker, we'll be on more nearly even ground.

The two Revenue Officers who had spotted him bumbled around like dancing bears as they tried to blend into their surroundings. Lance had to bite his lips to keep from laughing out loud at them. He didn't have long to laugh. He had just reached the Sports Section when a seasoned surveillance agent strolled by the tax-collecting clowns and shooed them away. The fact that they hustled off down the street and out of his view told Lance the A-team had arrived.

Reading the Sports Section gave Lance the opportunity to glance around for all of his watchers; like bananas they come in bunches. Lance checked his imaginary watch again and turned around to toss his paper into one of those mesh, metal trashcans the City of New York provided in the nicer neighborhoods. That housekeeping chore gave Lance a

360-degree sweep of the area, without the appearance of alertness. A no-frills government car sat behind a delivery truck a half a block behind him. Now Lance had the edge; he knew they were there.

He remembered when a client failed to tell him she had warned her husband that she was going to have him followed.

What a disaster! I'm not invisible, so he had no difficulty making it awkward for me to stay with him. Now I'm in that guy's shoes, except I'm not being followed by just one private investigator. Whittaker would deploy a team. How many? Is Whittaker with them? I hope he's here. At least one of them was hiding behind a truck in a grey Chevy sedan. That could be him.

If the surveillance team knew he was on to them, they would call for more agents and, given enough of them, he would not be able to pick them out of the crowd. Hell, they could form their own crowd!

Lance kept reminding himself: *Don't look directly at them; pretend you don't see them.* That is harder to do than it sounds. It is also difficult to walk slowly while excited by your full bladder and your uncomfortable situation. When Lance ambled up Madison Avenue, the IRS car didn't move right away. It would take over if he got into a taxi or on a bus. So long as he walked, foot surveillance would stay with him.

Move your eyes; don't turn your head.

Lance window-shopped to check his back from the reflections in the glass. A short, chubby guy behind him, and a tall thin one on the sidewalk across the street, signaled one another when they didn't think he could see them.

After a few blocks, Lance noticed the sedan had caught up, pulled into a bus stop, and then moved up, again.

What do I know about them so far? They aren't using radios. How do I know that? Elementary: If they had radios, the car would have paralleled me on another avenue. It would not bring up the rear where I might see it.

What else? So far they have only one car on the surveillance; if they had more than one, the cars would leapfrog, taking turns. I wouldn't be able to see the same car move each time.

Anything else? Until they get more help, there are only three of them. That's my educated guess. The two footmen on opposite sides of the avenue aren't rotating with fresh faces.

About fifteen blocks north on Madison Avenue, the art galleries started to dominate the storefronts.

Lance crossed the avenue and strolled into a residential street against the one-way traffic. That forced the surveillance car to circle the block and pick him up at the other end.

White marble stairs extended down to the sidewalk from the front doors all along the block of brownstones. Narrow concrete steps went down under them to doors that had once been service entrances, but were now front doors to basement offices and apartments. As he walked along the north side of the street, Lance read the plaques on the doors above and below his eye level, looking for a boutique business he could drop in on.

The short IRS guy ducked behind a stone staircase each time Lance turned his head to read a plaque, but Lance caught him in his peripheral vision.

The tall guy on the south side of the street walked ahead. Few people realize you can follow someone from in front. Lance was one of them— and so, apparently, was the tall guy.

When Lance reached Park Avenue, the IRS car was there.

Lance got a quick look at the driver as he started across the wide, divided avenue. He walked right in front of the Chevy's grill. The driver glared at him. He had the leathery skin tone one would expect of a Texas cowboy.

Must be Whittaker. In Manhattan we are exposed to the elements much more than most Americans because we walk from place to place, rather than drive. But the sun is hotter in Texas, and here the tall buildings give us so much shade we don't develop much of a tan.

When Lance reached the center island of Park Avenue, home to waist-high flower gardens, the traffic light changed.

The short, chubby man had to run to avoid the unleashed traffic in the southbound lanes, and had to stop and stand right next to Lance until the traffic cleared enough for both of them to proceed.

The taller of the two footmen had made it all the way across on his side of the intersection.

The IRS car could not have turned left from the right lane in the heavy traffic, even if the street had been one-way in that direction. Lance heard it burn rubber as it took off, and he figured Mr. Whittaker would try to find a way to meet him at the next corner. Lance also heard heavy breathing right next to him. He glanced right and gave the short guy a smile. Verbal pleasantries with strangers are not normal in the Big Apple.

The IRS fellow beside me is tense, as though I were a serial killer. He wasn't reassured by my friendly smile.

New Yorkers don't take orders from light bulbs, so as soon as Lance saw a hole in the traffic, he skipped across the northbound lanes. Again, he checked the upper and lower level plaques on the brownstone buildings.

His shorter follower gave him a head start since the taller one was on the other side of the avenue waiting for Lance to catch up.

There was a plaque Lance saw that he liked on a lower level door: Dr. Dinwiddie, Podiatrist.

What the hell, my feet hurt. Hope they have a men's room available.

Lance crossed the street, marched right in, and didn't look back.

The IRS surveillance team won't come in and make inquiries about me until after I leave.

Lance gripped the change in his pocket so it wouldn't jingle and glided, unnoticed, through the empty waiting room and down the hall. It was devoid of a men's room, and at the back door he was confronted with a sign that warned: *Do Not Open Door -- Alarm Will Sound.* Sure enough, there was an alarm bell bolted on the wall next to the door. It was attached by wires to the doorframe.

No sense alarming anyone, but I've got to go.

Muffled voices and movement in the rooms nearby tweaked Lance. He looked around and debated with himself: *Should I trip the alarm or try to defeat it?*

An empty Styrofoam coffee cup had been left on top of a fire extinguisher on the wall.

Perfect.

Jammed between the edge of the alarm bell and the wall, the soft cup solved the problem. Lance opened the door and exited while the muffled bell rattled away, too quietly to be heard.

Getting out of the backyard proved to be another challenge. Lance picked his way through unlocked gates and climbed over a low wall before he found a narrow passageway between two buildings that led to Lexington Avenue. He peeked out between a tailor shop and a travel agency, then walked to a corner coffee shop where he could study Dr. Dinwiddie's street without actually being on it. The stale breakfast smells of hash browns and onions grilled hours earlier still hung in the air as Lance passed through to the men's room in the back. Fortunately it was unlocked, and he didn't have to negotiate with the staff to get the key, otherwise he might not have made it in time.

Two minutes later, a much calmer Lance Walker sipped a coffee and studied the street. He spotted the taller IRS footman, but not the shorter one, nor the government car.

Suddenly, the Whittaker-suspect swung the IRS car around the corner and rolled down toward Dr. Dinwiddie's office.

Wonder what took him so long? Maybe he had to make a pit stop, too.

Whittaker parked beside a fireplug, across the street from the good doctor's place, and next to the taller agent.

Lance watched them and called Janet from a pay phone in the coffee shop.

"Good morning. May I help you?"

"Anybody looking for me?"

"Your shrink called," said she.

"Is this old home week, or what?"

"I didn't know you were seeing a shrink." Janet couldn't conceal her concern. She waited for an explanation, but when Lance didn't reply, she grudgingly continued. "Anyway, he said it is *critical* you see him right away."

The short round IRS guy rejoined his colleagues by the government car.

"Last thing I needed today," Lance told Janet.

"Someday are you going to tell me what that's all about?"

"Nah." Lance hung up the phone.

He had met the enemy and they were pretty good; without forewarning, he would never have seen them.

CHAPTER NINE

Shrink Rap

• • •

A Lexington Avenue bus swooped past the windows toward the bus stop fifty yards south of the coffee shop. Lance bolted out the door and sprinted to catch it while the IRS guys were still in conference, and no reinforcements had arrived to help them saturate the neighborhood.

Seven blocks later Lance got off the bus.

Bus fare reduces my taxable income to $23,717.67.

Lance walked two blocks farther east to a modern high-rise apartment building where a shrink he knew practiced psychiatry on the thirty-fifth floor.

Moments later, Lance reposed on a big, firm couch, stared at the blank, white ceiling in a totally silent room, and told the good doctor, "Gee, Doc, rotten reality notwithstanding, I don't feel too bad. What's wrong with me?"

Doctor Matthew Powell chuckled from the overstuffed chair behind Lance's back. "Nothing is wrong with you."

"What's wrong with *you*?" Lance tried to crane his neck around enough to see his client in the dimly lit room.

"*Nothing* is wrong with me," said the shrink with the patience peculiar to his profession.

"Then why the hell am I here? Have I overused my long-distance telephone privileges on your phone?"

Lance charged his calls to Doctor Powell's telephone to prevent the IRS from obtaining a list of all the long distance numbers he called. The doctor's telephone records were protected by the legal privilege patients have with their psychiatrists. Even if the IRS got the list of his calls, they couldn't ask Doctor Powell which were his and which were made by Lance. Answering that question would violate the doctor's ethical duty of confidentiality, and no doubt the doctor would warn Lance.

Doctor Powell said, "I owe you a lot more that the cost of a few phone calls. And now I have a critical problem with a patient."

He's never used the word "critical" before when he asked me to investigate one of his patients.

Lance said, "Another violent fantasy you want me to check out?"

The last two patients whose stories worried the doctor were a mousy stockbroker who said she was a weekend whip-tease queen in Greenwich Village, and a respected clergyman who told the Doc he had tracked down and murdered all his childhood friends. Lance verified that prissy Miss Wall Street did, indeed, flog the snot out of submissive guys at a fem-dom club every Saturday night. He also discretely ascertained that the preacher's playmates of yesteryear were all still alive and well.

"Worse than just a weird fantasy," the doctor said, "I prescribed medication to a depressed alcoholic patient, who remains anonymous; he paid with cash and I have no way to contact him." Doctor Powell paused, and paused.

Lance finally filled the silence with an unintelligent "Uh-huh."

The psychiatrist went on, "A recent study concluded that depressed men with this particular patient's chemistry, and given those two particular drugs in combination, destabilize and vacillate from manic to depressive, to suicidal, to homicidal."

Sounds like a chemical time bomb.

"You can't wait for him to come in?"

"No. I need you to find him as soon as possible." For the first time since Lance had known him, Doctor Powell sounded frightened.

Lance said, "Describe him."

"Well, his deep-seated guilt derives from a strict Catholic education. He grew up in 'White Harlem.' I don't know if that is a place or a state of mind ---"

"It's a place: Inwood. What's his name?"

After a pause, the doctor said, "He called himself *Jack*, but he slipped a few times while telling me about his childhood, and I think his true name may be Sean."

There must be an unwritten rule that all New York Irishmen are required to be known as Jack or Sean.

To get the doctor talking again, Lance asked the obvious, "Irish descent?"

"Well, his hair is bright red and he has a bit of an Irish accent, second generation, I suppose."

Lance supposed along with him. "Age? Height? Weight?"

"Jack is forty-four-years old. He's about my size. While his hair is bright red, he's starting to gray around the edges and, oh yes, he has freckles."

Now we're getting somewhere.

Lance asked, "Is he a morning person or an evening person?"

At what time of day can I approach this homicidal drunk and not get myself killed?

"Well, I would think he would be more exuberant in the morning and more morose at night."

Morning sounds safer to me.

"Anything else?"

There was a long silence while the doctor thought about it.

Wonder if Doc has fallen asleep?

Doctor Powell finally said, "Not that I can think of right now. Do you think you can find him?"

This is another case with "dismal disappointment" written all over it. If I had to bet, I'd put my money on "Jack" finding his way to a morgue, or a hospital, or a criminal court, before I find him.

Lance tried to sound upbeat. "Basic law of physics, Doc: Every *body* has to be somewhere."

CHAPTER TEN

The Setup

• • •

On the elevator down to the street, Lance thought: *It's too late in the day to look for Sean, also known as "Jack," and too early to go back to Times Square to look for Jennifer. I don't know what the hell I can do to investigate the Drysdale libel case, so I guess I should try to put a move on Mr. Whittaker and his IRS gang.*

Lance took the Second Avenue bus down to the lower East Side, mentally marked down his earnings to $23,716.17, and sought out a public telephone that wasn't busted. When he finally found one that still worked, he wiped off the earpiece with his handkerchief and called Janet.

While his phone in her office rang, he looked around at the rundown neighborhood. This was once the most densely populated place on earth, the second staging ground for most foreign immigrants back when Ellis Island in New York Harbor was their point of entry. Once they entered the land of the free, most of them moved to the lower-eastside. The rents were low and there were others of their ethnic origin with whom to share their gut-wrenching experiences. They tried to change their language and attitude to fit into this country, which seemed so strange and new to them. Few succeeded, but their children were Americans, and their ethnicity was added to our melting pot, right here, where the lumps still floated on the surface.

"Good Afternoon," Janet answered. "May I help you?"

"Any messages?"

"Not right now."

"'kay."

Lance disconnected with a flick of his finger, called information, deducted fifty cents (the cost of two phone calls) got $23,715.67, and asked for Doctor Dinwiddie's office telephone number. His quarter came back so he didn't have to deduct again while he dialed the good doctor.

"Doctor Dinwiddie's Office," a woman answered.

"Hello. My name is Walker."

"Mr. Walker," she bit off her words, "as I have already told that fellow from your office, twice, Dr. Dinwiddie is not taking any new patients. I don't know where you got the idea that you had an appointment."

No doubt in my mind who called her, twice. The IRS surveillance guys have tried to confirm I'm still in there.

"I'm sorry, Ma'am. My office probably made the same mistake I just made."

"Mistake?"

"I've evidently called the wrong Dr. Dinwiddie."

"There's only one Dr. Dinwiddie in Manhattan."

"Right," said Lance, as he hung up.

Hope she was as hostile to the IRS guy who made those pretext calls.

A stroll through the maze of four-story brick buildings (which are still walk-up apartment houses for new immigrants) brought Lance to the block which is the home turf of Satan's Savages motorcycle gang. A long row of Harley Davidson Easy

Riders were parked along one curb, and no vehicles were parked on the other. Anyone ignorant enough to park there would be in immediate danger of serious body damage to both their car and their person. Halfway down the block of low-rise brick buildings, on the motorcycle side of the street, is a sign with a skull and crossed bones, and the words: Satan's Savages Headquarters. Lance didn't enter the block. He hailed a taxi and instructed the driver to take him up the East River Drive.

The hack license identified the driver as Jihad Mohamet Shabaz. His name, accent, and deranged driving style marked him as a recent Middle Eastern immigrant. Lance had him get off the East River Drive at Seventy-second Street and cut over to Park Avenue, then north, again, past the west end of Dr. Dinwiddie's block.

The chubby IRS guy lurked near the Park Avenue end of the block with his foot up on someone's front step.

I guess he gets lower back pain, too. He didn't see me; he's facing Dr. Dinwiddie's door. They think I'm still in there being treated, under an alias.

The guy Lance thought was Whittaker stood behind the IRS car across the street from Dr. Dinwiddie's office. He wore cowboy boots and looked old enough to retire.

Jihad Mohamet Shabaz was confused by Lance's directions to "circle the block." When he turned South on Lexington Avenue, Lance said, "Drop me at the coffee shop on the corner."

As they approached, Lance saw his tall shadower leaning on the side window of the coffee shop watching the sidewalk in front of Dr. Dinwiddie's door. He didn't see Lance in the back seat of the taxi.

Hope there's still no more than three of them out here.

As the taxi drove through the intersection, Lance caught another glimpse of his pick for Group Supervisor Whittaker. Fast-food wrappers littered the street at his feet.

At least he has eaten. Maybe that put him in a better mood.

Lance told Jihad to wait and then hopped out of the cab before the cabbie could stop him. He darted into the coffee shop and positioned himself at the far end of the counter so the tall IRS agent at the side window couldn't see him if he looked inside.

"What'll you have?" a tubby guy in a food-stained apron asked as Lance rushed by him. Before he answered, the counter man delivered coffee and a donut to a tall thin Black woman in a New York Police uniform.

"Give me four coffees to go," said Lance, "One black, one light-no-sugar, and two regular."

The chunky, bald guy in the stained, white clothes stopped and poured the coffees into white paper cups with blue Greek columns and Amphora urns printed on them.

I wonder why every coffee shop in New York uses the same Greek-motif coffee cups. Maybe because the mafia "sells" them.

Lance turned to the female police officer and said, "There's a guy parked on a fire plug around the corner."

She raised her eyebrows but didn't look at him. She sipped her coffee as though Lance weren't there.

"He's been littering the street," said Lance.

No response from Ms. New York's finest.

"Take your time, finish your coffee, he's been there all day."

She slowly turned her face in his direction. Her hard brown eyes defied Lance to say one more word.

With four Greek-design cups of coffee in a small cardboard tray, Lance waddled to the taxi out front. He deducted the $4.32 in *tax preparation expenses* from his net receipts and got $23,711.35 in current taxable income.

Jihad Mohamet Shabaz was delighted to see him again; he had been stiffed before.

The one-way street pattern would have required a six-block drive to get back to this same corner, so Lance persuaded Jihad to back up through the intersection and then turn right to take him down Dr. Dinwiddie's block.

The tall IRS agent saw Lance in the cab when the Middle Eastern maniac made that insane maneuver.

Jihad dropped Lance right in front of the guy standing by his car. Lance slipped the kamikaze a fifty-dollar bill and said, "Should anyone ask, you picked me up right there at the coffee shop."

Jihad rubbed the big bill with his thumb and forefinger, smiled, and said, "Whatever you say, boss."

That's fifty dollars in "tax preparation expenses" off my taxable income, leaving $23,661.35 on which I owe income tax.

To make sure Jihad understood, Lance said, "You definitely did *not* pick me up at Satan's Savages Headquarters."

Jihad nodded. "Right, boss."

Lance got out of the taxi and walked around the government car to Whittaker.

CHAPTER ELEVEN

The Confrontation

• • •

"Mr. Whittaker," said Lance.

The pitter-patter of the taller IRS agent's feet behind Lance grew louder.

Whittaker did a double-take. Then he shouted to the short IRS agent at the other corner, "Stop that cab!"

Good move, Mr. Whittaker!

Lance said, "You should know that here in New York, *regular coffee* means coffee with cream and sugar. I've got one here that's just black coffee, like *y'all* drink it down in Texas."

Whittaker looked doubly dumbfounded. Lance not only knew his name, but he also knew he was from Texas.

Lance saw the chubby IRS agent stop the taxi and start to interrogate the driver.

Hope I didn't over-bribed Jihad.

The tall IRS agent arrived beside Lance, panting.

Whittaker recovered his equilibrium and bellowed, "Arrest this man!" He pointed at Lance.

My truce negotiations are not going well.

"What for?" asked the tall, breathless agent.

Whittaker bared his fangs and barked, "Bribery!"

"No one took the coffee yet," said Lance.

But that fact didn't delay the demagogue. "*Attempted* bribery!"

"You can be bought with a cup of coffee?" said Lance.

In his fury, Whittaker couldn't get his next sentence together. "I mean ... I mean ... I mean ..."

"Attempted *Gratuity*?" asked Lance, with his eyebrows raised.

The tall IRS agent informed his boss, "The U.S. Attorney here will not prosecute for a cup of coffee."

That encouraged Lance. "Go ahead and arrest me. The last time you guys hauled me in, the judge came very close to granting me an injunction against further IRS harassment." That was one of Lance's favorite fantasies, but not the truth.

Whittaker slapped the cardboard tray right out of Lance's hands. The coffees, *black*, *regular* and *blonde*, all splattered on the side of the IRS car, the cardboard tray, plastic tops, and Greek cups scattering on the sidewalk at their feet.

How did I plan to get out of this if making nice didn't work? I guess I don't have a Plan B.

Windshields are far larger than rearview mirrors because looking ahead is far more important that looking behind. Lance had a good memory but that didn't make him a superior planner. Perhaps it prevented him from thinking far enough ahead.

Lance just stood there, like a poster boy for Alzheimer's.

Whittaker grew angrier and angrier—for a very long, tense moment.

An authoritative female voice interrupted his stalled thought processes. "I'm citing you for littering." It was Ms. New York's finest from the coffee shop.

She listened to me after all!

"Look, Lady," Whittaker said, "I'm a Federal Officer."

He talked down to her. Big mistake.

"I don't care if you're the King of friggin' England, pal." She hauled out her ticket book.

"How would you like your taxes audited?" snarled Whittaker.

Big BAD mistake.

"How would you like to be busted for Disorderly Conduct?" said the cop.

The chubby IRS agent arrived at the scene of the squabble and looked as horrified as his tall counterpart.

The policewoman wrote Whittaker a ticket. "Here's a citation for parking on a plug." She handed it to Whittaker.

He growled and tore the ticket to shreds, which he then sprinkled on her sturdy shoes.

"This one is for littering." She started writing another ticket.

Good opportunity to un-ass the area.

Lance slipped around the corner of Lexington Avenue while Whittaker's subordinates tried to negotiate with the angry officer. The last Lance heard, she sounded just as implacable as Whittaker had been with him.

In a crowded butcher shop, Lance ducked down and pretended to study the specialty meats in the display case in order to hide behind the line of customers.

While the jurisdictional conflict played itself out around the corner, Lance peeked between the knees and hips of the folks who had taken numbers, until he saw the Mutt & Jeff, IRS team rush around the corner. They looked up and down Lexington Avenue, shrugged, and went back toward Dr. Dinwiddie's block. Lance waited twenty minutes to give his followers time to get out of the neighborhood. By then, women in short skirts were tugging at their hemlines before they stepped into his line of sight. He figured he had worn out his welcome and certainly didn't want to find himself confronted by the policewoman who worked this beat. She was already in a cranky mood.

CHAPTER TWELVE

Rush Hour In The Sex Trade

• • •

The subway took Lance back to Times Square and reduced his taxable income to $23,659.85.

A bagel and a regular coffee in the press of the afternoon pedestrian rush passed for lunch.

The Times Square hookers and hookerettes rushed to service their horny, but hurried, commuter clientele. Lance trolled the neighborhood and marveled at the perversion of the mating process.

Females trade sex for food, among birds and animals as well as humans, Nature's way for females to select males who can provide for them and their offspring. It also allows the most resourceful males to spread their seeds among the most fertile females. It's perfectly natural for a healthy young Playboy centerfold to marry a wizened old octogenarian, 62 years her senior, who just happens to be a Texas oil billionaire.

But here in the fetid meat market of Times Square, fecund females sell themselves to any stranger with a few bucks in order to support their drug addiction, their alcoholism, their pimp, or simply themselves. The sole thought of posterity, which occurs to either party to these tainted transactions, is that there shouldn't be any progeny.

Lance felt relieved that he didn't see Jennifer Lee among them. He also felt very vulnerable. He could have been under IRS surveillance and would never have seen them in the crowd.

FOREWARNED

Wonder if Mr. Whittaker's chubby agent got Jihad-the-cab-driver to tell him I hailed the cab right outside of Satan's Savages Headquarters? Whittaker and his gang might have more than they can handle if they try to interrogate the rulers of that temple of testosterone.

The battleship-gray sky still refused to drop its acid rain on Time Square, despite Lance's deep desire to see some of the perverts flushed away, along with their germs, viruses and fungi. If the weatherman were up for re-election, Lance would have voted for his opponent.

Lance's patience ran out.

Time to pick up a fresh package of laundry for me and some overpriced flowers for the lovely lady who's cooking my dinner, while I'm spying on sexy girls half her age.

CHAPTER THIRTEEN

Age-Appropriate Playmates

• • •

It was dark by the time Lance reached the monolithic brick apartment building in the West 80s, a remnant of the Great Depression when labor was cheap and the need for housing was acute. The Doorman-Porter-Furnace-Stoker, another remnant of the Great Depression, sat and smoked in a guard booth in the marble-lined archway entrance. He called Helen Karris and got her permission to let Lance go up to her apartment.

Lance's knock on the big, solid door in the big, solid building was answered by the little, solid widow, Helen Karris, a spirited redhead on whom middle-age spread looked good. Behind her stood another mature beauty, who looked nervous.

Oh no! I've been ambushed! No doubt Helen invited me over to meet her girlfriend, or cousin, or whatever she is.

Lance handed the pretty bouquet to his grinning hostess and felt like a little boy at his first dance. Worse, since he had his clean clothes tucked under his arm, he felt like a teenage boy on his first visit to a bordello, although these ladies, dressed in their casual best, looked far too neat and clean to be women of commercial passion.

"Come in. Come in. How you been?" said Helen.

"Making a living," said Lance, as he crossed her threshold.

"But are you making a *life*?" Helen kissed him on the cheek.

The other woman wilted a little under his gaze; she looked as anxious as he felt, and for exactly the same reason. No one enjoys being thrown together with a stranger of the opposite sex, like two members of the same species at the Bronx Zoo.

"There's someone here I want you to meet," said Helen. "She needs a man like you."

Helen was trying to make this easy for them. Her heart was in the right place, but her set-up had the reverse effect.

Lance cleared his throat before he spoke to the silver-haired woman who shivered behind Helen. "Ma'am, I'm sure you're a wonderful person, but I'm really not looking to settle down."

His bluntness embarrassed both women.

Helen's friend studied her shoes.

"In fact," he said, "after dinner I've got to go see some folks who don't show up for work till after midnight."

That was a bit too blunt. It sounded like I think they expect me to bed Helen's attractive accomplice before the clock strikes twelve.

"I'm not trying to fix you up," said Helen. She paused, then said, "Sophie ---"

"Sofia," her curvaceous cohort corrected her without looking up.

"Sorry," said Helen. "Sofia has a problem, and I think you might be able to give her some good advice. That's all."

Nice save, Helen! She has cooked up a good cover story to justify putting us together. They call that "plausible deniability" in the intelligence biz.

Sofia lifted her head and, despite her embarrassment, her countenance was still the most beautiful female face Lance had seen all day.

Fine, delicate features. Very pretty. No—gorgeous!

She said, "Let's feed the man, Helen, before we make demands on his time and talent."

And feed him they did. The widow Karris stuffed him with tasty avgolemono, delectable dolmades, and succulent lamb spanakopita. He washed it all down with retsina, a Greek wine that tastes of resin, but really enhances the taste of Greek food.

Of course the ladies ate too, albeit with less gusto than Lance.

Then Helen presented baklava and strong fresh-ground coffee.

Seated between the middle-aged enchantresses, Lance noticed that each smelled as crisp and clean as a fresh-cut cucumber. He said, "Helen you are a superb cook."

Helen nudged him and said, "You think *I* can cook? You should taste Sophie's cooking sometime. She's a wonderful cook."

Sofia leaned forward, peeked around Lance, and said, "Helen, don't start." Then, close to Lance's ear she said, "Look, I was married to a cop for twenty-seven years. When he died, I expected to receive his pension ---"

"It would have been a good pension too," said Helen, "more than I'm getting."

Lance turned his head to face Helen.

Sofia said, "Another woman showed up with proof that she married Marty when he was in the Navy, before I ever met him ---"

Lance swung back around to Sofia, but Helen said, "It's got to be a scam."

Sofia said, "I thought so, too, but she's got solid proof they were married."

Helen said, "Marty never told Sophie he'd been married before."

Lance's head was swinging back and forth like a spectator at a tennis match.

Sofia said, "At first I couldn't, but now I can accept the fact that he was married before—but it's just that he never told me about it."

"She wouldn't have married him if she knew he'd been married before," said Helen. "Sophie's a good Catholic—like *you* need…"

Lance ignored the hook on the end of that line.

Sofia said, "I'm not such a good Catholic." She paused for a breath and a moment of thought, then she said, "This woman, Wanda Sedgwick, says that Marty deserted her, and they never got divorced, and she's still, legally, Mrs. Martin O'Shea."

"And the cops wouldn't do anything about it!" said Helen. "They just gave the tootsie Sophie's pension."

"What could they do?" asked Sofia. "If *she* was legally married to him when I married him, then *my* wedding doesn't count—*legally*."

"That's not right," Helen said to the widow O'Shea. Then she asked Lance, "Do you think that's right?"

Lance finally got a word in. It was, "No."

While he had the floor and could rest his neck for a second, he asked Sofia, "You think Marty may have divorced Ms. Sedgwick somewhere?"

"I'm sure of it," she said. She patted his thigh under the table, not a sexy pat, just a touch to keep him facing her direction. Women can pat men if they want to, even though men can't touch women without permission.

Helen said, "Of course he did! You didn't know Marty O'Shea! If you knew that man, you'd know he was no bigamist."

Lance didn't turn to face Helen. He kept looking into Sofia's soft, brown eyes and asked, "Have you tried to find a record of the divorce?"

"Have I ever!" she said, "I hired a law firm ---"

Helen said, "They took every cent she had and never found anything."

Lance maintained eye contact with Sofia. "Have you tried Marty's Navy records?"

"The law firm got them for me," said Sofia. "The records show that Marty married Wanda ---"

Helen said, "And she got a good allotment while he was in the Navy."

Helen poked the back of Lance's shoulder with her finger to get his attention. Women can also poke men whenever they want.

"The Navy records don't show a divorce," said Sofia.

"Do they show where he was stationed?"

"He was stationed all over." .

Lance said, "Well, a foreign divorce ---"

Helen poked his shoulder again. When he glanced back at her, Sofia patted his thigh, and got his attention back. She moved so close he could feel the warmth from her body.

Helen yelled, "All over the United States!" and poked him again.

Sofia patted and said, "He was a Navy recruiter and ---"

Helen poked and said, "Spent his entire Navy career on dry land."

Lance felt like a puppy in obedience training. He asked Sofia, "Did the law firm check the divorce records where he was stationed?"

She said, "They tried, but ---"

"Those lawyers couldn't find French fries at McDonalds!" said Helen, with another poke. Lance almost turned his head.

Sofia patted and added, "They said there are thousands of courts where he could have filed. They couldn't check them all."

Helen said, "Because Sophie ran out of money!" She punctuated her exclamation with her finger poking Lance's shoulder.

Lance preferred Sofia's pats to Helen's pokes.

Sofia said, "They checked the logical courts, but ---"

Helen said, "She sold her house to pay those jackals!"

"They did the best they could," said Sofia.

Lance addressed the lovely lady patting his thigh. "The police can't help?"

"Lot of help they are!" said the poker.

"No," said Sofia. "You see, no one is sure where Marty and Wanda may have lived after he got out of the Navy and before he came back to New York."

"Even the Mafia wouldn't help!" said Helen.

"Helen!" said Sofia.

Lance snapped his head back and forth and saw the ladies give each other meaningful looks.

He said to Sofia, "You asked the Mafia to help?"

She said, "I come from a Mafia neighborhood in Brooklyn ---"

Helen said, "Vinnie Manarino's in love with her!"

"Helen!" said Sofia.

"Vincenzo Manarino?" said Lance, "the Capo?"

"I know Vinnie from the old neighborhood," Sofia said softly.

"He's in love with her," said Helen, "trust me." She pecked out the rhythm of her words on Lance's shoulder. "Vinnie Manarino never got over Sophie."

"That's not true, Helen," said Sofia. "Everybody in the old neighborhood got over Sofia," she patted Lance pleasantly, "especially when I married an Irish cop."

"Vinnie was glad to see you again," said Helen, "even after all those years."

What a surprise; Vinnie Manarino does not entertain.

Lance asked, "You got an audience with Vincenzo Manarino?"

"I was desperate," said Sofia, "and he won't talk on the phone."

Helen said, "He said he was happy to receive the only woman he's ever truly loved."

Lance asked, "He said that?"

"He's Italian," said Sofia, as though that explained everything.

"What did Vincenzo say he could do about your problem?" asked Lance.

"He said I married a cop, so let the cops find the divorce case."

Helen said, "Vinnie told her she could marry him and then she wouldn't need Marty's pension."

Lance looked to Sofia for confirmation.

Sofia said, "Nobody needs a pension in Vincenzo's line of work."

Lance said, "I have an idea, but I really have to talk to you about it alone." He turned to Helen.

She looked surprised at first, but recovered fast. "Oh. Look, I want to catch the eleven o'clock news, if you two will excuse me."

"Thank you," said Lance and Sofia in unison.

Helen rose and crossed the room to her bedroom door. "Just leave the dishes on the table," she said.

"We won't be long," said Sofia.

Helen turned on the television in her bedroom. Lance could see the screen through the open door. A dog food commercial provided good covering sound.

Lance lowered his voice and said, "This has to be a secret between you and me."

"Okay," said Sofia.

"How do you feel about Vinnie Manarino?"

"He's the scum of the earth."

"Good, 'cause it's a big mystery about how Vinnie got so powerful. I was in jail with his cousin years ago and Vinnie wasn't nothin' then. You have any idea why he's a Capo now?"

"Yeah. It's his uncle, his mother's brother from Sicily. He put Vinnie in charge of payoffs in New York."

"What's his uncle's name?"

"I don't know. I met him once, but that was years ago."

"Tell me about when you met him."

"Helen told me about your memory. I don't have a memory like yours."

"Everybody has a memory. Just relax. Close your eyes. Take a deep breath."

She closed her eyes, filled her large lungs and breathed out slowly; her shoulders sagged.

"Take another."

Her head tilted back and her abundant chest arose as she complied.

The commercial on Helen's TV ended and was replaced by the news. The anchor man said, "It's Eleven O'clock, New York, and this is how it looks from here."

"Another deep ... slow ... breath," said Lance in a deep ... slow ... voice.

FOREWARNED

A picture of Satan's Savages Headquarters appeared on the TV screen behind the talking heads. The area was littered with overturned garbage cans and upset Easy Riders. The anchor woman said, "There was some excitement this afternoon at the New York Headquarters of Satan's Savages motorcycle gang. The police Civil Disturbance Unit was called in to quell a near-riot resulting from an Internal Revenue Service attempt to serve a summons on the bikers' club."

Holy cow!

"Relax," Lance said softly to Sofia, hoping his excitement about the news didn't ring in his voice.

The graphic on the screen was replaced by a police officer, clad in riot gear, who said, "Without casting dispersions, I think I can say we consider this a violence-prone neighborhood. We routinely visit here in force."

The female reporter asked, "Had the IRS been warned about the gang's propensity for violence?"

The policeman said, "The Department provides escort for sworn members of other agencies who need to conduct business in violence-prone neighborhoods."

"But the IRS ignored your warnings?"

"It's my understanding that the Internal Revenue official involved was newly transferred here from Texas."

Whittaker!

The reporter's voice asked, "Was he badly hurt in the riot?"

"I never used the word 'riot,' ma'am," said the policeman. "We're calling this a minor civil disturbance."

"Was the guy hurt?"

"Define 'hurt.'"

The news desk in the studio came back on the screen. The anchor said, "The IRS declined to confirm or deny that any of their personnel were in today's punch-up, citing a section of the Tax Code which forbids disclosure of tax information. Sources at Ballinger Orthopedic Hospital tell News Three that one IRS agent was admitted with broken bones and a concussion."

At least Whittaker didn't get Mutt & Jeff busted up.

The widow O'Shea was waiting for Lance to notice her. She was watching him watch TV.

"Sorry," he said. He got up and closed Helen's bedroom door. When he returned to the table, he said, "Close your eyes again."

She did.

"Recall the time when you met Vinnie's uncle from Sicily."

"We had just sat down to eat," she said, in a sleepy voice, "when this whole herd of wise-guys came in with this little old Sicilian man ... they were all fawning over him ... treating him real important ... Vinnie jumped up and hugged him ..."

"What did Vinnie say?"

Sofia's chin sunk down to her chest. She murmured, "Vinnie … said … 'Sofia allow me to present my Uncle Giacomo Braccole.' That's it!" Her eyes popped open. "Or were we eating broccoli?" Her eyebrows furrowed.

"Don't talk yourself out of it," said Lance. "How did you find out that Uncle Giacomo put Vinnie in charge of paying bribes?"

"Vinnie's mom. She wasn't supposed to know, but she was *so* proud."

"'kay," Lance said. Then he made his pitch.

"Look, with me in the middle, I can minimize the risk to you, but this plan is still very dangerous."

Sofia said, "One thing I learned from Marty: You can't let the bad guys scare you."

CHAPTER FOURTEEN

Sex Workers' Night Shift

• • •

The Doorman-Porter-Furnace-Stoker's eyes were glued to the screen of a round, basketball-sized, black-and-white TV in his little guard booth when Lance strolled out the marble archway.

It had rained. Lance decided to walk to Times Square. New York City is magical after a rain, tons of dog dung washed away, most pedestrians are still inside, and the smell of ozone is invigorating.

Too bad I can't deduct shoe leather or even rubber soles. The IRS says, "Normal wearing apparel is not a legitimate business expense."

Almost all of those three thousand Revenue Officers go home at five o'clock. There's little chance that one of them will spot me, at least not until I get to Times Square, where the sultry ambience might inspire a few of them to work a night shift investigating the vast untaxed profits of the sex biz.

The sounds of traffic mingled with the wailing of distant sirens as Lance strolled down Seventh Avenue.

In Times Square the streets were deserted, except for the hookers, their customers, and their pimps. Hookers on the night shift are those who can't sell themselves in daylight. The rain had knocked a dent in their cash flow.

Lance sauntered up to a gaggle of them huddled on the corner engaged in girl-talk. "Not much action tonight," said he.

The friendly females all agreed. A big blonde said, "Better get it while you can, Honey, no action at all tomorrow night." The others concurred.

"Oh? Why not?"

A chubby redheaded working girl said, "We'll all be at the Players Ball."

One of the streetwalkers spotted three tall pimps meandering their way from the next corner, patrolling their domain in colorful crushed velvet Edwardian suits, matching high-heeled shoes with four inch platform soles, and armed with jeweled canes. "Oh shit!" she said. "Here comes trouble."

All the girls clucked fearful comments.

Lance decided to talk to the pimps away from their women, so he advanced to meet them in their burgundy, green, and blue pimp suits. They stopped when they saw him coming their way. The tallest, Master Green, shouted, "What you want, man?"

Lance stopped and shouted back, "I want to talk to you, tall guy." Messrs. Burgundy and Blue both chuckled.

"I'm right here, man," the tall guy in the green suit bellowed, "get your butt over here."

Lance didn't oblige.

High heels clicked and girlish voices chirped behind him as the rash of hookers scattered.

"It's personal," Lance yelled back. "Step over here where we can chat, privately."

His two colleagues teased their spokesman, "He's in love with your skinny ass," said one.

"Better run right over there," said the other, "the man wants you, *now*."

"You want to talk to me?" the skinny whoremonger barked, "get your ass over here!"

Lance challenged his manhood, "Well, if you're too scared to talk to me without your two buddies ..."

That did it. The pimp charged Lance, brandishing his jeweled cane. "I'll show you who's scared."

"Oh, he's gonna kick some ass now," said one of his colleagues.

"Show him who's boss, Jimmy," shouted the other.

When Jimmy got within striking distance, he wind-milled the cane and swung it up from the sidewalk toward Lance's crotch. Lance caught it just short of his family jewels. The cane burned his bare hand like a fastball. Lance jerked it up in an unsuccessful effort to snatch it out of Jimmy's hand. The cane snapped in the middle, leaving each man with half.

Shocked, Jimmy looked at the shattered end of his half and said, "You broke my stick!"

"Could of been your neck," said Lance.

Jimmy jammed his free hand into his pants pocket.

Lance jabbed the splintered end of his short stick under Jimmy's chin, brought him up on his toes to even greater heights and said, "If that hand doesn't come out empty I *will* break your neck."

Jimmy swallowed audibly, his Adam's apple squiggling around the splinters, then slowly pulled his hand out of his pocket, empty.

"Now," Lance said in a friendly tone, "tell your associates that we're old friends, so they won't worry about you."

Jimmy's Adam's apple did another noisy somersault.

"My name is Walker, and I just want to talk to you for one minute."

Jimmy nodded as best he could with sharp wooden slivers stabbing his throat.

Lance lowered his weapon half an inch.

"Hey! This guy's Walter," Jimmy shouted to the two cane-toters behind him, "he's an old friend of mine, it's okay."

They said something Lance didn't understand, but he whispered, "Good. Let's walk around the corner to the all-night coffee shop."

"Won't let us in," said Jimmy, "no pimps allowed."

"That sucks," said Lance. "Come over here under the light and look at something."

Under a green neon sign in a storefront window, Lance showed Jimmy the photograph of Jennifer Lee.

"Seen this girl around here?"

"Yeah, but I can't tell you where she's working."

"Where did you last see her?"

"No, man," said Jimmy, "I can't tell you where she's working."

"You know where she's working?"

"I tell you where she's working," said Jimmy, "and you show up there after I be talking to you here, and I be dead meat, man."

"I promise you I won't show up where she's working."

"Pimps hear a lot of promises."

"I keep my promises."

"You keep your promises to a pimp?"

Lance reached up, hooked his hand around the back of Jimmy's neck and pulled his head down until they were nose to nose. "Yes. And I also promise you this: If you don't tell me what you know, I'll hurt you bad."

Jimmy gulped again. "She's working the phones at an outcall service. Arnie hasn't turned her out yet."

"Arnie! What kind of a name is that for a Mac?"

"Arnie Lipshitz? He's an NBA."

"Arnie Lipshitz? Basketball player?"

"No, Man, Business College, Arnie got hiself a NBA."

"Oh, an *M*BA. I guess he knows a good paying business when he sees one."

"Yeah, he sure know that."

"What's the phone number?"

Jimmy looked all around. "If I give you the number, you can find out where the place is at."

"I'm *not* going there. I'll just call."

Reluctantly, Jimmy took his address book out of his hip pocket, looked up the number, and read it out. He seemed surprised that Lance didn't write it down.

Five minutes later Lance dialed the number from a public phone in the all-night coffee shop, lowering his taxable income to $23,659.60.

"Escort Service Extraordinaire," a teenage girl's voice answered, trying to sound sexy, "How may I help you this morning?"

"Jennifer?"

She gasped, then recomposed herself. "Who is this?"

"I'm a friend of your grandfather, Lee," said Lance, "he'd sure like to hear your voice. His private line is ---"

She hung up.

Lance coughed up another quarter, reduced his income to $23,659.35, and dialed again.

This time an angry man answered. "Escort Service Extraordinaire, good morning." His greeting sounded like a threat.

"Arnie?"

"Yeah. Who's this?"

"A friend of Jennifer's grandfather. Do you know she's only fifteen?"

"No shit." He wasn't shocked.

"*Any* work Jennifer does for you could mean big trouble."

"In that case, you won't catch her answering my phones anymore. I've got work off the premises she can do."

"Her grandfather could make it worth your while not to employ her at all."

"Worth how much of my while?"

"He might be willing to go five thousand—if I ask him nice."

Arnie chuckled. "You're going to have to ask a lot nicer than that."

"How much nicer?"

"I couldn't let her go for less than fifty thousand."

"Fifty thousand!"

"That's just half of what she'll net over the next year."

And I thought I was good with numbers!

"I'll see what I can do."

Back at Helen Karris's building, the Porter-Doorman-Furnace-Stoker's snores echoed in the marble archway when Lance slipped by. The old man reeked of cheap alcohol.

CHAPTER FIFTEEN

A Little Taste Of Ireland

• • •

Lance was snoring on Helen's couch when Sofia woke him the next morning.

Helen giggled in the background.

"Wake up and smell the coffee," said Sofia. "Looks like you had some night."

"I've got a busy day, too," said Lance.

No IRS agents were visible on Lance's route to the subway that took him to Inwood, and left him with $23,657.85 to pay taxes on.

Inwood is the northern-most neighborhood on the island of Manhattan and it's off the grid, because it's on terrain too hilly for regular streets. With limited street access and surrounded on three sides by water, it is easy to feel you're no longer in New York City, or even the United States. If the voices on the street were all Lance had to go by, he might well have thought he was in Ireland, an unlikely place for the IRS to frequent, but Lance stayed alert.

He spotted the first pub on his mental list, *The Waxies' Dargle*, named for an Irish ditty that Lance whistled as he approached the door. The song commemorates the annual picnic of Dublin shoe-makers (*waxies* because they used wax to seal the seams) at a park on the Dargle River, not far from Donnybrook, once the site of an annual fair that usually ended in fisticuffs. Thus, today, a punch-up is sometimes called *a Donnybrook.*

If there were a bar called "The Donnybrook," I would have gone there first. More to Sean's liking, I'm thinking.

As it turned out, Sean, also known as Jack, was not drinking his breakfast at *The Waxies' Dargle.* Only elderly drunks sat at the bar. They all looked up when Lance entered. It might as well have been midnight in Death's waiting room: the yellowish light coming through the dirty windows, the stench of stale beer, and the wizened old faces combined to give the place a surrealistic air.

"Has me lad, Sean, been in this morning?" Lance used his brogue to ask the young bartender.

"Sean!" the bartender yelled to the row of sodden, old men.

Four of them pushed back from the bar. They had black, brown, gray, and white hair.

"Right over here," said the one with dyed-black hair.

The guy whose hair was brown held up his hand and asked, "What do you want?"

"I don't know him," the gray-haired Sean said to the bartender, referring to Lance.

"Did you want me?" said the Sean with white hair.

"The Sean I'm looking far is a bit younger," Lance said to one and all. "He has red hair and freckles."

"Beats me," said the bartender as he dried a beer mug with a bar towel.

Dyed-black Sean said, "Sounds like the lad who caused that entire ruckus over at The Derry."

"That guy never drinks in here," said brown-haired Sean.

Sean-the-gray said, "I don't know him," still referring to Lance.

"Lots of Seans in the world," said Sean-with-the-snow-on-top, looking around at the three Seans surrounding him.

Lance asked black-topped Sean, "Well, would you be knowing his last name?"

"Nah," said he.

Sean-o-brown said, "You'll find no infarmers here, bucko."

Lance's next stop was the Derry City Pub. The now familiar smell of stale beer was overwhelming. The jukebox played a rousing Irish rendition of "The Patriot Game," and the morning drunks looked Lance over while his eyes adjusted to the low light level.

"Has me lad, Sean, been in this marning?" asked Lance.

The grandmotherly bartender said, "He was in yesterday, buying rounds for all and sundry, but suddenly he went berserk and ---"

"Over nothing a'tall," said one of the drunks at the bar.

Another said, "We was just talking about how he flew out of here," then paused to burp, "but none of us could ---"

"Do you know where he lives, then?" asked Lance, "I'd like to pay him what I owe him before I drink i'tall up."

"Downtown somewheres," said the old woman bartender. "Any of yuz know where Sean lives?"

The morning beer drinkers all mumble negative responses.

"I don't even know his last name," said Lance.

"Anybody know Sean's last name then?" the bartender asked her customers.

They didn't.

Lance handed the bartender a twenty-dollar bill, mentally reducing his taxable income to $23,637.85, and said, "Give each of the lads one for me. I've got to go find Sean before I start drinking."

The bartender announced, "He's buying yuz all a round!"

The old men blessed Lance and all the children he ever had or might have.

"Do you think you'll be seeing Sean again soon?" Lance asked the bartender, the only sober soul in sight.

"Not after that fracas he started in here yesterday," said she.

"Would ye be after giving me a call if he comes in, then?"

"If he ever shows up again, I'll mail him to you—in wee small packages."

Lance took his leave with a loud farewell, "Top o' the morning to all of yuz."

"And the rest of the day to you, sir," said bartender.

Lance found a public telephone and called his favorite psychiatrist, leaving $23,637.60 as his current income.

The shrink answered promptly and Lance asked, "Do you think Sean will come back to the same bar where he caused a scene?"

"No. I wouldn't think he would ever return to a place where he embarrassed himself."

At the third Irish pub Lance visited in Inwood, he found Sean sitting at the bar telling a funny story to several dissipated old men surrounding him.

"So, no matter what the Head Master did, the two boys just hated each other more and more ..."

Sean seemed out of place, much too young and well-dressed to fit into this wretched brotherhood of aged boozers. There was some sort of blue ticket sticking out of his shirt pocket. It had numbers and letters on it.

"... One of the boys grew up to be an Admiral in the Royal Navy," said Sean, "and the other became a Bishop ..."

"What'll it be?" the beer-bellied bartender asked Lance.

Lance dropped another twenty-dollar bill (now he owed income tax on $23,617.60) and said, "I'll have a beer, and draw a round for the lads at the bar."

The tubby man in the white apron drew the beers as Sean's story went on.

"... One day the Bishop arrives at Paddington Station wearing his frock, of course, and he spies his old schoolmate, who is wearing his Navy Admiral's uniform..."

The barman took beers to everyone around Sean.

"... The Bishop pretends he doesn't recognize his oldest enemy. He shouts to the Admiral, 'Boy! Would you fetch my bags, please?'"

The bartender waited politely for the story to end, but the attention of the audience was drawn to the fresh beers.

"The Admiral cheerfully takes the Bishop's suitcases and says, 'Of course I'll take your bags, ma'am. A woman in your condition shouldn't be carrying anything heavy.'"

The old drunks laughed dutifully, but couldn't keep their eyes off the beers.

Sean was annoyed that he'd lost their attention, just when he wanted it most.

Passing out the beers, the bartender said, "These are from that fellow," nodding toward Lance.

The customers hoisted their full mugs and expressed their gratitude.

Lance raised his own mug right back at them. "Hup the rebels!"

As the drunks around Sean return cheerful Irish toasts to Lance, he could see Sean quietly changing from Dr. Jekyll to Mr. Hyde.

"May the road rise to meet you," said an old man, just before he burped.

"Hup the freebies!" said another, paraphrasing the salute.

One right next to Sean shouted to Lance, "God bless you, lad!"

"You think I'm a rebel?" Sean asked angrily, he was talking to Lance.

"Nah, man," said Lance, "it's just an old Irish toast."

The burper said, "I'm an old Iris toaster," and laughed at his own joke.

Mr. Grateful-For-Freebies said, "Hup the tall ladder and down the shart rope ---" He paused to down a short beer.

"--- to Hell with King Billy and God save the Pope," screeched the one who earlier invoked the Divine blessing on Lance.

Sean staggered toward the door, his empty beer mug in hand.

Lance was watching him in the back-bar mirror. As he passed behind him, Sean raised his arm and smashed his beer mug on the back of Lance's head.

Flash bulbs went off in Lance's brain. He felt nauseated and dizzy for a moment, but heard Sean say, "We were having a grand old time till you showed up and ruined i'tall."

By the time Lance regained his feet, Sean was gone.

The sumo-sized guy behind the bar handed Lance a stack of bar napkins. "Here, you're bleedin' in the back."

Lance dabbed the bloody spot on the back of his head and said, "Anybody know that guy's name?"

Burpy said, "*Sean* something."

Freeby said, "Nah, Paddy, it's *Tom* something." He was lying.

"Anybody know where he lives?" asked Lance.

"After what he did to you," the bartender said, "we couldn't tell you where to find him, even if we knew."

The drunk, who had blessed Lance, said, "It would lead to farther bloodshed, you know."

Lance staggered down Nagle Avenue to the Dyckman Street station and stumbled down the stairs of the IRT subway, pressing the blood soaked napkins to the throbbing mound on the back of his head. He didn't even look around for the IRS.

CHAPTER SIXTEEN

Fashionable First Aid

• • •

The crowded subway car lurched along on screeching steel wheels. Still woozy, Lance repeatedly subtracted $1.50 subway fare from $23,617.60 and got $23,616.10, every time. The other passengers tried to keep their distance from him because he looked like a bloodied bozo with a bar napkin compress.

When Lance entered the fashionably funky hair salon, two receptionists looked at him like cats look at a ball of yarn. Behind them, trendy hairdressers tended customers amid music, conversation, glasses of wine, and the strange humming sounds emitted by the equipment. The color pink was everywhere.

"Do *you* have an appointment," asked the receptionist with iridescent orange hair and matching low-cut top.

To her right, the bright green-haired receptionist in the bright green dress giggled at the very idea that he might. She wasn't as bright as her choice of color.

Lance said, "I'd like to get my hair washed."

"A shampoo is fifty dollars," said the orange gal, "by appointment only." She poked up her smug face, and her perky breasts rose to the occasion.

"I'd like Pinky to wash my hair," said Lance.

Both receptionists laughed.

Ms. Orange said, "I'm afraid ---"

"Mr. Pinky's the owner," said Ms. Green.

Her colleague said, "He doesn't shampoo ---"

Ms. Green said, "We have Shampoo Techs ---"

"Just tell Pinky I'm here," said Lance.

"*Whom* should I say is calling?" asked Ms. Orange.

The green-haired receptionist giggled uncontrollably.

"Lance Walker."

Ms. Orange dialed the phone.

Ms. Green noticed the blood stains. "Yuck!" she said, "blood on your collar."

Lance said, "I've got blood in my hair, too."

"There's a Mr. Lance Walker here, sir," Ms. Orange said into the telephone.

Ms. Green said, "Why didn't you rinse the blood off before you ---"

"Sir!" the lass with the phone said, "he's got blood in his hair!"

The other dizzy damsel said, "Maybe you should see a doctor."

Ms. Orange said, "He wants *you* to shampoo him."

"We just do hair here," said Ms. Green, "not wounds."

"Sir? ... Sir?" the other girl said into her telephone.

"What did he say?" Ms. Green asked her colleague.

"He hung up."

"See!" Ms. Green told Lance.

Just then, Pinky strode in from the back and gave Lance a bear hug. "Walker! My old friend. So good to see you."

The receptionists looked like patients undergoing electro-shock treatments, which actually might have done them both a lot of good.

"What the hell happened?" asked Pinky, as he looked at Lance's battered brain casing.

"A beer mug."

"Holy Cow! Let me wash it out."

"That's half of why I'm here."

The receptionists were still vibrating as Pinky took Lance to the back. He shooed a Shampoo Tech out of a stall, put Lance in a pink chair, and eased the back of his injured head down into a pink sink.

"When you got out of jail," said Pinky, "I never thought I'd see you again."

Lance said, "Last time I saw you, you'd just been hit with a twenty-year sentence."

"Yeah. Thought I'd do it all, too." He rinsed out the dried blood with warm water. "Feds got no sense of humor when it comes to pimps."

Lance shifted around trying to get comfortable. "How'd you get out?"

"God bless those dope dealers. They overcrowd the prisons, and we less-dangerous felons got evicted to make room for them."

Pinky gently lathered around the lacerations.

"I see you got out of the procurement racket and into the hair biz," said Lance.

"Yeah, I got reformed. How did you find me?"

"I saw your ad at the bus stop."

"Good." Pinky rinsed Lance again. "Glad I bought that ad. You still snooping for a living?"

"Yeah," Lance chuckled, "*I* never got reformed."

"You said this blood in your hair is only half of why you're here?"

"Right."

More shampoo bubbled through Lance's locks.

"What's the other half?"

"The Players Ball."

Pinky laughed. "You going?"

Lance laughed too. "If I can find where it's at."

"This year, tonight, the Players Ball is at the Saint Bernard Hotel."

"That old dump? Good place for it."

"Even better," said Pinky, "It's now owned by wise guys."

"Why am I not surprised?"

"Guess who runs it for them," asked Pinky.

"Who?"

"Remember that little guy, Marino? Smuggled a crowbar into a bank? Got caught busting open safe deposit boxes?"

"Crowbar?"

"Yeah, Crowbar."

CHAPTER SEVENTEEN

Unpleasant Feds

• • •

Lance's next two stops were a laundry and a drycleaners where he freshened up his attire to match his squeaky-clean hair.

Then he took a subway, which reduced his taxable income to $23,614.60. None of his fellow passengers seemed to notice him this time. He got off at the first stop in Brooklyn and walked across Cadman Plaza to the Federal Courthouse where he found a door marked, *Organized Crime Strike Force*, and let himself in.

The reception area wasn't much bigger than a decent phone booth. A video camera hung from the ceiling, pointing at three rickety chairs and a stack of government forms. Behind a bulletproof window, a Strike Force agent in shirtsleeves looked up from a paperback novel and said, "Fill out one of doz forms and I'll be right wit chew."

"I'd like to talk to someone about Vincenzo Manarino," said Lance.

"Just complete one of doz forms."

Lance particularly didn't want to put his name on a piece of paper there. The Task Force probably had IRS agents on board, and even though Whittaker's bounty offer was probably unknown to them, after the blow to his head, Lance was more than a little paranoid.

"No. I don't do forms. Tell whoever's interested in Manarino I'd like to talk to them."

"All of us here are interested in every one of da greez balls."

The agent didn't look important enough, or sound qualified enough, for Lance to confide in him, but he had no choice.

"Okay, I want to propose a deal. If you'd like to know where Vincenzo Manarino gets his power ... his family connections ---"

"Who are you?"

"I don't want my name in your records—at least until I know we have a deal."

"We don't do deals with anonymous people. You could be working for Manarino, or you could be wanted for something. What's your name?" His demanding attitude made Lance feel like a frightened fugitive.

"Forget it." Lance turned to leave.

"Wait a second, pal." The agent stood up.

Lance looked back, shook his head at the bureaucrat and reached for the door handle.

The man behind the bullet-proof glass must have already pressed some sort of alarm button, because when Lance opened the door he found himself confronted by three large federal agents. They weren't wearing their suit coats so the big handguns and little radios on their belts were visible proof of their authority.

"Can we help you, sir?" asked the one in front.

Lance said, "I doubt it."

The guy behind the glass said, "He refuses to identify himself."

His three pals pushed Lance back inside and closed the door. They patted him down and found no weapons.

"Am I under arrest?"

"You're under investigative detention," the smallest one explained. "You look like the kind of guy who knows what that means."

"And you look like the kind of guy who knows that resisting an illegal arrest is not a crime."

The biggest agent smirked. "I'll just bet you know we can use necessary force."

"And I'll just bet you know that Federal agents can be sued, personally."

"What's your name?" the big guy demanded.

"What's yours?" Lance shot back.

"Bivens." The big agent smirked again.

Bivens -v- Six Unnamed Narcotics Agents was the case, started in this very courthouse, which determined that federal agents can be sued by injured citizens. Before that, federal agents were immune to lawsuits.

"Yeah, I bet." Lance pushed past the big three and marched toward the exit.

Since this was Brooklyn, Lance figured they would try to follow him to his car, get his tag number, and identify him that way. It might not occur to Brooklyn-based agents that he came by subway.

Lance crossed the street to Cadman Plaza. One of the feds followed. Lance pretended he didn't see him hiding behind a parked car, watching through the windows and chatting on his little radio. He trotted into the park when Lance reached the sidewalk on the other side.

A no-chrome government car burned rubber out of the courthouse garage and got stopped by the light a block behind Lance.

I must have really pissed them off, but what could I do?

It's a guy thing.

Lance angled back across the park, leaving the guy on foot dancing in the street, waiting for the light to change so the car could pick him up.

Lance took the opposite sidewalk right under the Brooklyn Bridge, climbed the stairs to the walkway on the historic span, and heard his pursuers roar under the bridge toward the Jehovah's Witnesses Watch

Tower. They were trying to pick him up on the other side of the bridge abutment. They apparently didn't think Lance would merely stroll over the old suspension bridge that was designed to accommodate pedestrians as well as horses and wagons.

CHAPTER EIGHTEEN

Pleasant Feds

• • •

At the other end of the mile-long Brooklyn Bridge is another federal courthouse, at Federal Plaza, across the street from the Federal Building in lower Manhattan. Lance nudged his way through people bustling in and out. A man on a crutch, with his arm in a sling, and his head wrapped like a mummy, caught Lance's attention when he hopped around in a circle trying to get a better look at him.

That might be Whittaker. The IRS offices are in the building.

Lance hustled to the elevators and took off before Hopalong could catch up.

He entered a door marked, *Federal Bureau of Investigation,* and found himself in a much nicer reception room than the one he just left in Brooklyn.

The pretty receptionist behind the bullet-proof glass stopped typing on her computer terminal. "May I help you?"

"I'd like to talk to someone about Vincenzo Manarino."

She looked at a long list of names on her desk and said, "He's not on my list of agents. Do you know what division he's assigned to?"

"He's not an FBI agent, he's a Mafioso. I'd like to talk to someone *about* him."

"Oh! He's a subject?"

Subject sounded so much more refined from the lips of an intelligent looking young woman in Manhattan than *greez ball* had less than an hour ago in Brooklyn.

She tapped a few keys on her keyboard, looked at the screen, then asked, "How do you spell the last name?"

"M - A - N - A - R - I - N - O."

She entered it, asked Lance to wait, and placed a telephone call. She put down the receiver and said, "Special Agent Bonsignore will be right with you."

"Bon-sin-YOR-ay" is Italian for "good guy." I like that.

Lance sat in an armchair, flipping through a magazine, upside down, wondering if the FBI agent would live up to his name.

A statuesque Nordic blonde woman in a smart-looking black pants suit entered the reception area. Lance fumbled the magazine and it fell on the floor.

She glided right over to him. The closer she got the better she looked.

"Sir? I'm Special Agent Bonsignore."

All FBI agents have *Special* in their title, but none of them had ever seemed so special to Lance as this one.

"You have something to tell me?" she asked.

Lance rose to shake her hand. "*Bonsignore* must be your married name."

She looked genuinely puzzled. "I've never been married."

Lance followed her to a small private office down the hall. Hell, he would have followed her to Los Angeles.

They settled in on either side of a table in the barren little room and he explained, "I have a friend who has known Vincenzo Manarino all his life. I can get you the inside dope on the guy, but I need two things from you."

"And they are?" Her cornflower-blue eyes were windows into a quick mind, despite the misleading camouflage of long pale-yellow hair.

"First, I want my friend protected. I don't want to be responsible for getting an innocent bystander hurt."

"Neither do I," she said sincerely.

"Second, I have an unrelated investigative problem."

Her forehead wrinkled. "What's that?"

"I'm trying to locate a divorce case, but I don't know where it was filed. I don't have people all over the United States, but you do."

"We're not private investigators. We only collect information for the government."

"Maybe you can think of a way to help me find the case I'm looking for."

"We can pay you for information and you can hire private investigators."

Lance wrinkled his nose at that suggestion.

I don't need any more income to pay federal taxes on.

"Let me put it another way," she said, "We can't give you information once it's in our files. Disseminations are proscribed by law."

"There must be a legal way you can consider my record checks official business ..."

She looked thoughtful. "Well ..."

"We can do it piecemeal." Lance leaned forward. "I can front you something now and, after you check it out, you can check court records for my divorce case in, say, California."

She leaned forward, too. She smelled as good as she looked. "How will you know when we find the divorce case you're looking for?"

"You'll tell me."

"If we tell you, we might never hear from you again. What makes you think we will let you know when we've found it?"

Smart lady.

"I'm a fair judge of people, Ms. Bonsignore."

Up close, eyeball-to-eyeball, he felt he was, literally, in a position to judge.

"Call me Gloria," said she.

Lance said, "You wouldn't string me along—Gloria. Besides, when you find that case for me, we can cut a new deal."

Gloria said, "You'll have to front me something before I decide."

"Don't ask me how I know this, but Vinnie's Uncle Giacomo Braccole, a mafia Don, traveled all the way from Sicily to the U.S. of A. just to put his favorite sister's son in charge of paying bribes."

The name "Giacomo Braccole" seemed new to her; she jotted it down.

"I'll check it out," she said, "but even if it means something, all of California is too much to ask for this little information sample."

Special Agent Bonsignore drove a hard bargain, but she had the advantage of not lusting after his body while they haggled.

Lance tried not to let it show, but he kept wondering what it would be like to spend a night in Gloria's place.

Lance said, "I'll settle for a check of all the divorce courts in *Southern* California for the dissolution of the marriage of Wanda Sedgwick and Martin O'Shea. All I want you to do is tell me which court it's filed in. I can go get it once I know that. Of course, this divorce matter has nothing to do with my secret source of information about Vincenzo Manarino."

"Don't tell me that," she said as she noted names of the erstwhile divorcees, "I might have to say it *does* have a lot to do with your secret source of Vincenzo Manarino information, in order to justify checking divorce records."

One more thing to worry about, well two, counting his personal concern for Gloria Bonsignore's private life.

CHAPTER NINETEEN

Whittaker's Lair

• • •

Lance was so pleased with his new professional relationship that he didn't notice a guy picked him out of the crowd in the lobby of the Federal Building.

"Excuse me, Mr. Walker?" said the middle-aged, average-looking civil servant.

"Yes."

"I'm Inspector Levine with the IRS."

"Yes?"

Lance was still too high on Gloria Bonsignore's aura to think straight.

"Can we talk?" Inspector Levine gestured toward the elevators.

"Go ahead." Lance didn't move.

"My office is upstairs—if you don't mind."

Levine's office was an unremarkable windowless box which smelled of cheese, clean, uncluttered, and uninspired.

"I understand you had a run-in with Henry Whittaker," said Inspector Levine.

"Yeah. He didn't care for coffee."

"I guess he's leaning on you pretty hard right now."

Lance shrugged.

"How did you know his name, and the fact that he came here from Texas?"

Suddenly, Lance noticed a little red light on the intercom and realized they were not alone in this conversation.

No doubt Henry Whittaker, himself, is listening in on our little chat.

Lance said, "Wait a minute!" and pointed to the intercom. "That's why we're here, rather than downstairs."

"What?" Inspector Levine put on his glasses.

I guess he thinks I won't punch him with his glasses on, or maybe he just wants to look more official.

"You didn't invite me up here to ask about Whittaker's ---"

"Allegations of misconduct by an IRS employees are ---"

"I haven't made any allegations—yet."

"It has come to my attention ---"

"I've heard you IRS guys get investigated when you don't press hard enough to generate complaints."

"That's not entirely true."

"But it's partially true?"

"Just tell me how you knew Whittaker's name," he said in the tone of a demand, "and the fact he just came from Texas."

"What you really want to know is how I knew what Whittaker was up to."

"There's a Federal law," Levine said threateningly, "Title 26 of the United States Code, Section 6103, which makes it a felony to get information out of the IRS."

"I'm no lawyer, but I'll bet that law is intended to protect tax infor ---"

"It's in the Tax Code."

"--- not illegal tactics by IRS personnel."

"Let the lawyers argue about the statute, perhaps at your trial, if you chose to be the test case."

"See you in court, *Schmuck!*"

Lance rose to leave, but paused long enough to say, "In fact, the Federal Whistleblower Statutes would probably protect any IRS employee who disclosed that Whittaker posted a bounty on a taxpayer. You're wasting your time, tough guy."

It's amazing how indignation sharpens your thinking. A great idea hit Lance right after he *didn't* hit Inspector Levine. But he wouldn't want the beautiful Ms. Bonsignore to hear he had beaten up a federal agent, right in her building.

But to tell the truth, Lance did punch a mousy looking IRS agent once, years ago, and the Revenue Officer turned out to have mastered the ancient martial art of Akido. He calmly told Lance all about it while he tied him up with his own arms and legs. The tax man could have broken all his bones, but he didn't break any, his admirable self-restraint had rubbed off on Lance, the hard way.

CHAPTER TWENTY

The New York Public Library

• • •

Lance's heightened hostility, a good idea, and the Lexington Avenue subway carried him to Grand Central Station. He deducted the cost of the subway token, got $23,613.10, and walked two long blocks along Forty-second Street to the Main Branch of the New York Public Library. Stone lions guard the wide-open stairs to the marble halls of accumulated learning.

Time to try to solve young Barkley's problem.

In the cavernous Research Room, cluttered with quietly busy people and reference books of all description, Lance spotted a sign suspended from the ceiling: *Research Librarian.*

On approach, Lance discovered two librarians behind a desk serving two lines of people. Lance got into the shorter one, which led to a petite woman in her thirties who had striking blue-gray eyes. Her voice was pleasant too. She patiently told the gal in front of him, "The new edition of *Who's Who In Leather* hasn't come in yet, but we expect to have it within the week. Perhaps you can check back with us."

Lance noticed the woman was clad in form-fitted, lightweight, tan leather apparel, tastefully done.

"If you could give me your phone number," the leather lady said, "I'll call first to make sure it's here before I come in."

There was no number on the old fashioned telephone on the research librarians' desk.

"Sorry," the woman with the wonderful eyes replied, "we can't give out the extension. If we provide phone-in service for one person, we would have to do it for everyone."

The animal-skin wearer nodded and clicked away smartly on tan leather high heels.

Lance stepped toward the big desk, only to be cut off by a guy in a wrinkled suit, who seemed to think whatever he wanted was more important than anything Lance did.

"Where can I find ---"

"I'm sorry," the lovely librarian interrupted, "this gentleman—" she pointed to Lance "—is next."

The rude man snorted, eyed Lance as though he were a leper, then stepped behind him, muttering, "I just have a simple question."

"Sir?" The tiny woman's hypnotic eyes were aimed at Lance.

"Thank you," said Lance. "Is there a British businesses newspaper which competes with the *London Leader*?"

"The *Crown Commercial Courier*." Amazing the stuff librarians know by heart.

Lance said, "The *London Leader* has an Investigative Reporter, Michael Slyker. Does the *Crown Commercial Courier* have his counterpart?"

"I'm sure I don't know, but you can look for yourself." She pointed to a stack of newspapers on the shelves right behind her. "You'll find both the

London Leader and the *Crown Commercial Courier* in that rack right there."

"Thank you." Lance stepped over to the papers and heard the librarian ask the bad-mannered guy, "May I help you, now?"

The newspapers were stacked upside down for a normal reader, but Lance flipped through them the way they laid. It was faster that way.

The arrogant fellow said, "Where can I find the current roster of the New York Yankees?"

"You could ask my son," the librarian said, jokingly.

"Is he here?" No humor in his question.

There! In Lance's hand, a front-page story in the *Crown Commercial Courier* by Investigative Editor Martin Gerrard.

Lance heard the librarian tell the baseball bully, "If you want a roster that's really accurate, as of today, you can call the New York Yankees offices and they will be glad to give you one."

"Good idea!" First pleasant sound out of him.

Lance heard the baseball fan's fading footsteps as he pondered what sort of man "Investigative Editor Martin Gerrard" would turn out to be. Then Lance heard his librarian tell her colleague, "I wish he *could* ask my son. The Yankees are all Travis talks about."

The other librarian asked, "You take Travis to the games?"

"Yeah, sure," Travis's mom said, sarcastically, then changed her tone to wistful. "Wish I could afford to. He'd never forget it."

CHAPTER TWENTY-ONE

A Foggy Call To London

• • •

The two-beep tone of a British telephone ringing in London pulsed in Lance's ear. Luckily, Lance used a pay phone behind the Gothic windows in the lobby of the Lincoln Building. The traffic noise outside would have made this difficult call impossible from a pay phone on the street. Of course, Lance charged it to Doctor Powell's telephone credit card.

"Crown Commercial Courier," a switchboard operator answered.

"Good evening," said Lance, in view of the five-hour time difference. "I know it's late in London, but is Martin Gerrard still in the office, by any chance."

"Not 'by any chance.' Sometime I think he sleeps here, in a file drawer. Hold on, caller."

The next voice Lance heard answered, "Gerrard."

"Hi. Just called to ask why the Crown Commercial Courier didn't cover the Drysdale story, that appeared in the London Leader. Surely, you had the same information."

It was a long shot, but you never know what folks will tell you if you don't ask.

"Oh yes, but as I told that young man, 'You can't make bricks without straw.'"

"Uh-huh," Lance said, unintelligently, wondering who *that young man* might be, and what the hell he meant by "you can't make bricks without straw."

"Apparently, I was wrong," Gerrard said. "Slyker over at the *Leader* published it, without the straw."

"You said, 'young man' just now. Was that a figure of speech? Didn't you mean the 'old man from New York'?"

If the disinformation agent wasn't Connolly, who the hell was it?

"No, Drake can't be more than thirty."

"Drake?"

A light bulb switched on over the head of the man 3,459 miles away. "Oh! ... I mistook you for someone else ... now I understand what you're doing... well, that terminates this conversation." And it did.

Hearing the disconnect tone, Lance, too, hung up, but he was smiling. He looked around the dark quiet lobby, then dialed again.

"Good afternoon, may I help you?" Janet answered.

"Anyone besides the IRS looking for me?"

"Lawyer Barkley wants to hear from you ASAP."

"'kay."

Although Lance was within easy walking distance of Norman Barkley's office, he decided to break the minimal news he had by telephone. He reached Barkley's prissy British receptionist, and she buzzed her boss, whose voice came on the line.

"Yes. Put him on. Mr. Walker? I hope you've got some solid evidence. I'm meeting Dan Tyler and his colossal legal guns in less than an hour."

"I don't have much—yet. A guy named Drake peddled the story in London."

"Who's Drake?"

Naturally, I was about to ask him *that question.*

"I don't know."

"Does he work for Tyler?"

"I don't know that, either."

"What the hell do you know about him?"

"Not much. He's probably about thirty. I said he was from New York and wasn't contradicted."

"This is disappointingly little with which to try to face down a guy like Tyler and his pride of lawyers."

"Yeah. Can you stall them?"

"Hell no! Any delay tells them how weak we are."

"I can't think of a thing I can do in an hour. It's ten o'clock in London, maybe I could reach Slyker."

"He gave you Drake's name?"

"No. I got that from Michael Gerrard."

"Call this Gerrard person back and offer him a hundred grand for all the details."

"That would blow up in our faces."

"Just do something!" Barkley bellowed and then slammed down his telephone.

Lance glared at the receiver buzzing in his hand. Two of the three people he had just called hung up on him.

I've got to work on my telephone manners.

Since his quarter came back after the Barkley call, Lance only lowered his net income to $23,612.60.

CHAPTER TWENTY-TWO

Friends In Low Places

• • •

The Saint Bernard Hotel looked out of place. A once pretentious palace was now dwarfed by glass boxes that could have come in kits at some gigantic Wal-Mart store, known only to architects. Walking into the lobby was like swimming into the Titanic at the bottom of the ocean. The glorious wood and plasterwork were severely deteriorated, and the first-class furniture looked too rickety and bug-infested to want to sit on, but Lance wasn't there for that. He was there to try to find Jennifer Lee at the Players Ball.

The desk clerk and the uniformed bellman hung together, leaning on either side of the massive marble front desk, and looking as seedy as their surroundings. They studied Lance as he drew near.

The desk clerk asked, "Something we can do for you, sir?"

"I'd like a room."

The desk clerk and the bellman looked at one another in mild surprise.

Lance asked, "You *do* have rooms?"

The bellman said, "Can I get your luggage for you, sir?" He was being sarcastic. Lance had no luggage, not even a package of clean laundry. He didn't intend to sleep here.

"I can handle it," said Lance, being just as sarcastic.

The desk clerk asked, "How many in your party, sir?"

"Just me."

"Will you be with us long?"

"Just tonight."

The clerk looked at his records and said, "Would you like a single with a Queen sized bed, or would you prefer the Honeymoon Suite? Those are the only two we have left."

"I'll take the single."

"How will you be paying for that, sir?"

Lance took out the packet of Mr. Lee's cash. "Promptly."

The desk clerk handed Lance a registration card and said, "If you will just fill this out." The clerk went to work on the world's oldest calculator. "The room will be three-hundred-seventy-four dollars, plus eight-point-two-five percent New York State sales tax, plus five percent New York City occupancy tax, plus two dollars per-person room occupancy tax ---"

"One person," said Lance.

The clerk punched it in and pulled the handle. "For a total of ---"

Lance said, "Four-hundred twenty-five dollars and fifty-six cents," while the ancient adding machine was still chunking.

The clerk's head popped up, looking as though Lance had just shot him in the chest. He would have been even more amazed had he known that Lance had also mentally reduced his total taxable income to $23,187.04.

"Local calls are free," the clerk muttered, "and long distance calls are nonexistent. You'll have to make them from someplace else."

Lance handed over the cash and said, "At these prices, I could stay in a suite at the Plaza."

Of course the Plaza would never host the Players Ball. The *players* pay top dollar just to be tolerated.

The desk clerk nodded, no doubt wondering why, at those prices, Lance chose to stay in a tacky room at the St. Bernard, rather than in a suite at the Plaza. "Here's your key, Mr. ---" He read what Lance had written on the card. "--- Walker."

The bellman said, "That's novel. Everyone else registered tonight is named *Smith*."

Lance asked the bellman, "A lot of cash check-ins today?"

The desk clerk answered for him, "None dressed like you. Room 414 is next to the elevators."

At nightfall Lance stationed himself near the ballroom doors to observe the players arriving. The dusty bulbs on the high ceiling cast an eerie yellowish light on the weird multi-colored creatures below.

A parade of Black, White, Hispanic, and Asian pimps, each accompanied by a cosmopolitan entourage of hookers, promenaded toward the ballroom. Pink plumage predominated in a sea of sequins on garish garments. Lance saw his friend, Jimmy, the tall pimp he had met in Times Square. Jimmy was decked out in his finest and armed with a new jeweled cane. When he saw Lance he looked away, but not before Lance caught the flash of fear in his eyes. Lance pretended not to notice him or his ladies, even though two of his woman smiled and waved at Lance.

Seductive music swelled from the ballroom. A big Black pimp, with skin like patent leather, mistook Lance for the hotel manager. "You better get some more people out front parking them limos," said he, "they's blocking the street."

"Right away, sir." Lance snapped his fingers and shouted to the bellman, "Bellhop!"

The shiny black pimp moved on with his whores.

The sarcastic bellman's face showed he couldn't believe his summary summons. "You talkin' to me?"

Lance smiled, shook his head, and waved him off.

The ballroom was nearly full. The parade was subsiding, and Lance was still there by the door studying the sex-sales convention. No sign of Jennifer Lee.

Suddenly, a hand clapped down on his shoulder. Lance spun around and found himself nose-to-nose with a solid looking White pimp in a green suit. Lance didn't know who he was, at first.

"You're blocking our big entrance, man," the pimp said in the tone of a threat as he pushed Lance aside and arranged his bevy of bimbos.

When Lance saw Jennifer Lee, he knew this pimp must be Arnie Lipshitz.

Among Arnie's ladies, Jennifer was the youngest, least confident, and dressed least like a prostitute, in a blood-red, Spandex mini-dress, so tight that, even in this light, anyone could see she wore nothing under it. The only other thing she wore was a pair of shiny six-inch heels in a matching crimson color.

She stuck to Arnie Lipshitz like a frightened puppy.

He told her, "You bring up the rear, Babe." She looked disappointed to be shuffled to the back of the pack. "Ladies," Arnie said, and then strutted into the ballroom to the beat of the tantalizing music, a high-class harlot on each arm, followed by the rest of his provocative party. Jennifer bumbled to the back.

"Hi, Jennifer." Lance slipped his arm around her. "Let's take a hike."

Her reaction was less compliant than Lance had hoped. She screamed bloody murder and fought to break free of his grasp.

"Arnie! Arnie! Arnie!"

Arnie's brood tried to intervene as Lance hauled Jennifer toward the elevators, the clutch of clucking call-girls fluttered around him, clawing and chirping for "Arnie!"

Lance tucked Jennifer under his arm. She kicked and screamed and flailed, but Lance had a good grip around her waist. She wasn't going anywhere without her midsection. Struggling got her horizontal and she swam a furious free style in the air, ripping the dresses of three of her would-be rescuers. Her flying feet knocked two of the grasping whores off their very high platform shoes.

Once in the elevator, Lance pushed the pursuing prostitutes out, then simultaneously pressed the *Close Door* button and the one marked "3" with his free hand.

Jennifer kept kicking. Her fetish pumps pounded the wall, and her shrill screams threatened to puncture his eardrums in the confined space.

Arnie ran out of the ballroom and raced past the tarts fiddling with their torn dresses. He hurdled fallen women, but just as he reached the elevator doors, they closed in his face, shutting off the sounds of the hubbub Lance had caused.

Starting with button "3," Lance's finger ran up the row of odd-numbered buttons. No need for Arnie and his pimp pals to know exactly which floor he was going to.

Jennifer's incessant screaming finally got to him, and he gave her bottom a stinging smack.

"Quiet!"

Shocked into silence, she still squirmed as hard as she could.

"If you scream," said Lance, "someone will call the cops, and the cops will return you to your parents."

The logic got through to her. "Okay," said she.

As the elevator reached the third floor, Lance put Jennifer on her feet. He discretely held her by the back of her neck as the doors opened on a Black pimp and his ladies. They all smiled at Lance and Jennifer, unaware of the events below.

"Going up?" asked Lance.

"No, man," said the pimp, "We're all going down." How true. His ladies snickered as the elevator door closed them out.

Jennifer rubbed her hip and said, "You can't just take me away from Arnie."

"I just did."

She stuck her lower lip out like a porch on her face. "Not for long."

"Long enough for a chat."

She eyed Lance like an alien.

When the elevator stopped on the fifth floor, Lance pulled Jennifer out and pushed her into the stairwell. She was reluctant to be liberated.

They could hear the hoof-beats of pimps galloping up the stairs below them.

Lance muffled her mouth with one hand, twisted her arm behind her with the other, and forced her down the stairs to the fourth floor landing. Lance troubled to peek around the door before he shoved her into the hall.

No sooner had the door closed behind them than they heard the stair-climbers thunder by on their way to some higher floor.

Lance pushed Jennifer into his room and locked the door.

Wonder how long it will take Arnie to beat my name and room number out of the desk clerk? Hell, the bellman would tell him for nothing.

Jennifer gave Lance an insolent snarl. "How do you plan to get me out of this hotel?"

I was just wondering the same thing.

"Look," said Lance, "I know you think Arnie is in love with you ---"

"I was sleeping in the bus station and starving when Arnie found me."

"To him, you're just an investment."

"He treats me like a lady! That's more than I can say for you!"

"Arnie offered to sell you to your grandfather."

"Oh, yeah," she said with a toss of her head, "Why didn't grandpa just buy me then?"

"'Cause I didn't tell him about the offer."

She looked puzzled.

Lance went on, "Arnie said he plans to make twice as much, after he turns you out."

Lance stared out the window while she thought about that. He figured he could get to the door before she could get it unlocked.

Apparently she thought so, too. She plopped down on the bed, and a whiff of dust puffed out of the bedspread.

"Call your grandfather. I'm sure the two of you can work things out."

"I don't know his number."

"Dial nine for an outside line, then 212-555-1689."

She picked up the heavy black Bakelite telephone, older than either of her parents, dialed, and asked for Mr. Lee. "Tell him it's his granddaughter, Jennifer."

Lance tried not to listen.

Pimps don't do anything until they've been paid. I wonder how much whip-out cash Arnie has on him, and how many cruel men with knives, straight razors and little nickel-plated pistols are combing the hotel for me right now.

Jennifer's side of her conversation with her grandfather intruded on his musing. "I know you love me, Grandpa, but Arnie loves me, too. No, no, Grandpa, Arnie really cares about me.

I mean, like, he smokes, but he made me quit smoking."

There was a sheer drop of at least a hundred feet outside the window, no fire escape, not even a ledge. A loud banging on the door snapped Lance out of his funk.

"Give it up Walker!" It was the voice of Arnold Lipshitz.

"Take a hike!" Lance replied.

Lance heard Jennifer whispering into the telephone. "I don't think we can get out of here."

"I know you're in there!" Arnie bellowed. Then to someone with him Arnie yelled, "Break it down!"

Most of the furniture in the room was bolted to the floor and walls. Even the base of the phone was glued to the nightstand.

At last, Lance grabbed the straight-backed, wooden chair and it came off the floor. He swung it like a baseball bat as he warmed up near the door.

Jennifer ducked down behind the bed, giving her grandfather a play-by-play description of the action.

Lance yelled, "Mr. Marino isn't going to like it if you bring the heat down on his hotel."

"Who the hell is Mr. Marino?" Arnie yelled back. Then he barked his order again, "Bust down the door!"

The weight of a couple of guys slammed into the door. No more than a second elapsed between the time the door bulged under the impact of the first guy and the second. Had they hit it at the same time, the old door would have splintered. Their bodies gave it another one-two punch, and then another, the antique wood was weakening.

Perhaps a well-placed fib might save Jennifer's life, and mine, too.

"I've got a permit for this nine millimeter! I got no problem with the police when I off you guys busting into my room."

The two bodies stopped bouncing off the door.

"Bust the fucking door!" bellowed Arnie.

"You fucking crazy?" a pimp yelled back at him.

"Just do it!" Arnie *was* crazy.

Behind Lance, Jennifer said, "I'll have to call you back!"

Arnie shouted, "You've got fifty-thousand dollars' worth of my property, Walker, and I want her back, right now!"

"Her family won't pay fifty thousand."

"Like I told you, if they don't pay, I'll take it out in trade."

Jennifer gasped.

Lance heard a guy in the hall ask, "What seems to be the problem?"

"Who the fuck are you?" Arnie demanded.

"I'm the guy who owns this hotel."

"Crowbar?" Lance shouted, hoping like hell that Crowbar wasn't all alone out there against a crew of armed pimps.

Crowbar sounded surprised that someone knew his prison name. "Who's that?"

"Walker."

"Walker! What you got yourself into?"

"Hey, Crowbar. Arnie out there wants his girl and we want to leave, that's all."

Lance heard Crowbar tell the pimps in the hall, "You gentlemen have to go back to your party now. My associates will accompany you to the ballroom."

The word "associates" flowed over Lance like a warm fuzzy blanket. Marino *did* have other Mafiosi with him out there.

One of the pimps must have menaced one of Marino's men with a handgun, because Lance heard a new voice say, "You shoot somebody with that piece of shit, you're liable to piss them off. But you shoot somebody with this—" Lance heard the pimp gasp "—and you blow their fucking head right off their fucking shoulders." Had to be a shotgun, probably sawed off, very popular with the mob because it's one of the few weapons one can purchase in New York City without a permit.

Arnie was stuttering, "But ... but ... wait a fucking minute! You can't let that guy steal one of my girls."

The sound of the elevator doors opening was followed by the thumping of pimps' bodies tossed into it by goons who considered them pansies.

One of pimps said, "You still owe us each five-hundred bucks." Had to be talking to Arnie. So did another who yelled, "And six-fifty for my fuckin' gun."

No sooner had the elevator door closed off the commotion than Lance's old prison pal, Crowbar Marino, shouted, "It's okay now, Walker."

Crowbar and two refrigerator-sized Mafiosi escorted Jennifer and Lance through the lobby. Arnie glared at them, but he was busy counting out cash to his pimp pals who had him surrounded. Pimps don't do nothing for nothing.

CHAPTER TWENTY-THREE

Top Of The Morning

• • •

Lance and Jennifer took a cab to the limousine service kept on retainer by her grandfather. Then they took a limo around Manhattan to insure they were not followed. By the time he got Jennifer safely back to the Lee mansion, Lance was bushed.

Jennifer and her grandfather were energized. They chatted enthusiastically in the plush parlor while Lance melted into an overstuffed chair.

"I wish you'd let me pay you, Mr. Walker," his long-time client said.

"For your granddaughter? Come on."

"I could never pay you enough for rescuing her, but I could, at least, pay you something."

"No, you can't."

Jennifer said, "Grandpa's going to take me to all the Yankees games. Could you come too?"

"That's right," the old man said. "I've bought a block of season tickets, and I've given a pair to every one of my clients. I'd love to give you a couple."

"Well ..." Lance didn't really care much for the Yankees, but how could he say that.

"Go on give him a pair, Grandpa. He can bring a friend."

"Of course," said her grandfather.

"Actually, I'd like two of those tickets. I know a little boy would love to go to all the Yankees games."

Mr. Lee picked up an envelope full of blue tickets, each with the section, row, and seat number printed across the end.

Lance closed his eyes and tried to remember where he had seen a ticket like that recently.

He could still hear Mr. Lee and Jennifer talking, but they sounded far away, far away from the Irish bar in Inwood, where Sean had tried to break his skull, but only busted a beer mug. Lance could see it in slow motion, the film running in reverse, backward from the impact on the back of his head, back to when Sean was sitting among the old drunks telling a joke about an admiral and a bishop, back to the blue ticket sticking out of his shirt pocket. A Yankees ticket!

What were the numbers on it? Let's see. Lean in and look at the end of the ticket, Section 14G, Row 141, and Seat Number 514. To confirm it, Lance ran his memory forward over Sean's ticket a second time.

"Give him more than two, Grandpa," Lance heard Jennifer say. "He's going to give those two away."

Lance's mind's eye zoomed back away from Sean. He was telling his funny story.

From that other dimension, Grandpa Lee said, "Mr. Walker is welcome to as many of these tickets as he wishes."

"Right," Jennifer said, "give him all of them. I bet he has lots of interesting friends."

"We should keep two, unless you've changed your mind about going."

The focus of Lance's memory had pulled back to the front door of the bar where he first saw Sean surrounded by the old drunks.

"No," said Jennifer, "keep two tickets for you and me. Would you like the rest, Mr. Walker? ... Mr. Walker?"

Mr. Lee said, "Mr. Walker, are you all right?"

Lance opened his eyes. His host and hostess looked concerned.

"Mr. Walker?" Mr. Lee said, again.

Jennifer asked, "Should I call a doctor?"

Coming out of his trance Lance tried to talk, but only grunted.

"Are you all right?" Mr. Lee asked, again.

"Oh. Yeah. I must have dozed off."

"You sure you're okay?" asked Jennifer.

"I'm too old to stay up all night with girls your age. I'm terribly sorry. I didn't mean to be rude."

"You're not rude," said Mr. Lee, "you're exhausted."

Wrapped around the tickets in Mr. Lee's hand, Lance noticed a letter on the stationary of *The New York Yankees Baseball Organization.*

"May I see that letter?"

Mr. Lee looked offended. "These tickets are perfectly legitimate, Mr. Walker." He handed Lance the letter.

"I'm sure they are, Mr. Lee."

Lance noted the telephone number on the letterhead and glanced down to the signature line: *Tuppence Goodwilli, Season Ticket Coordinator*. Who could forget a name like that?

"So you coming or not?" Jennifer asked Lance.

"Probably not, Jennifer, but I'd like two tickets for my friend and her son." Lance asked Mr. Lee, "Could I use your phone?"

"Of course."

As Lance dialed the vintage rotary-dial French telephone, Mr. Lee asked, "Would you like some privacy?"

"No," said Lance and he shook his head. Into the telephone, he said, "Tuppence Goodwilli please."

"What's he doing?" Jennifer asked her grandfather.

"I'm sure I don't know," he said with a curious smile.

"Hello, Ms. Goodwilli? I'm in a bit of a pickle. I have a friend's season ticket and I need to return it ... My friend's name is Sean, Sean Mc-something, one of those Irish names I can never remember. I need to give his ticket back to him, but ... The ticket number? Sure, I have it right here ..."

Mr. Lee and Jennifer looked at one another, bewildered.

Lance closed his eyes to envision Sean's ticket again. "Yes, here it is: Section 14G ... Row 141 ... Seat Number ... ah ... Seat Number ... ah ... I don't have my glasses on," Lance lied, "I think the seat number is 514 ... McInerny! ... That's right! Sean McInerny ... You wouldn't happen to have his address would you? I could just mail this back to him ... Two East Eighty-ninth Street. Okay! Thanks a lot Ms. Goodwilli!"

"What's going on?" Jennifer asked when Lance opened his eyes and hung up the phone.

"May I make another short call?" Lance asked her grandfather.

"Of course. Make all the calls you want."

While Lance dialed again, Jennifer said, "I don't get it."

Mr. Lee said, "Neither do I, and I doubt that Mr. Walker will explain it to us."

His sister, Janet, answered his telephone in her office. "Good morning. May I help you?"

"Anybody looking for me?"

"Just Lawyer Barkley, wants to see you as soon as possible today."

"'kay. Won't be real soon though, I'm tied up this morning."

"I'll tell him if he calls back."

"'kay."

Lance hung up, bounded out of his chair, plucked two tickets out of Mr. Lee's hand, and dropped the unused portion of his cash on the French writing table. It was still in the band marked: *$5,000.00*.

Lance said, "Here's the $4,500.00 I didn't spend."

The refund lowered his taxable income to $18,687.04.

"Oh, please, take it," Mr. Lee said, with a wounded look on his face.

"No chance."

Lance bolted out of the parlor, ran out of Mr. Lee's mansion, and beat feet to the high-rise home of his feisty foe, Sean McInerny.

CHAPTER TWENTY-FOUR

Defeating The Doorman

• • •

When the unformed doorman stopped him, Lance asked, "Is Sean up yet?"

"Sean?" The Puerto Rican doorman wasn't giving up any information voluntarily.

"Sean ... Uh ... Damn! I can't remember his last name," Lance lied. "And we were just drinking together last night. I must be hung over. Sean's an

Irish guy, mid-forties, red hair, little gray around the edges ... freckles ..."

"Sounds like *Four C*," the doorman muttered to himself.

"McInerny!" Lance said, "that's it, McInerny." Lance wanted to confirm that the doorman wasn't thinking of some other Sean who came in drunk last night.

The doorman looked up the name McInerny on his list. "Yeah, here he is, McInerny, Four C. I'll buzz him."

"No! Wait a minute. He's likely not up yet. A friend of ours is coming. Let's wait till he gets here before we rouse old Sean."

The doorman shrugged. "Okay, no buzz. Whatever."

"Can I use your phone?"

"No outside line here, but there is a pay phone on the corner over there."

At the public phone on the corner, Lance had to yell over the traffic noise on Fifth Avenue so Doctor Powell could hear him.

"Sorry to get you out of a session, Doc, but I think I have your loose cannon located ... No, no ... I can watch the place. Just finish up there and come join me ... Yeah. Bring that stuff with you ... Finding him was my job, getting him under control is yours."

A call to his number in Janet's office left Lance puzzled. She didn't answer his phone. First time that had ever happened. His quarter didn't come back, so Lance deducted that one as well, making his taxable income $18,686.94.

Twenty minutes later, Lance's psychiatrist client climbed out of a taxi just south of the corner—out of sight of the doorman. Perfect.

Lance joined him there while he settled up with the cabby. They had a brief meeting, so Lance could coach him.

Fortunately, Doctor Powell had a ring of keys he could use as a prop. Lance put the keys in the doctor's pocket, then pulled them out and shook them. Lance had him try it. He had to move his doctor bag to his left hand to smooth out the necessary key-handling maneuver.

Lance marched around the corner with the Doc ten steps behind.

Lance approached the doorman, who said, "I'll buzz Four C for you now."

"No. Not yet."

"Okay," said the man who was accustomed to dealing with nutty tenants and their strange guests.

Lance reminded him of their last conversation, about expecting another friend of Sean at any minute. "He said he'd be right over."

The doctor blew by them and the doorman tried to stop him.

"Sir?"

But the Doc averted his eyes, whipped out his key ring and jingled the keys as though he was looking for the proper one.

The doorman started after him, but Lance stepped in front of him, facing the other way, and exclaimed, "Wow! Look at that!"

The doorman skidded to a stop and turned to see what Lance was shouting about.

Lance looked frantically for something to point out.

The doorman whirled around and saw the elevator door close with the Doc inside. Duty delayed is duty undone.

"Will you just look at that!" Lance yelled, again. He had finally spotted something to talk about.

"What?" the doorman turned back toward the front door.

An unremarkable woman was walking a nondescript dog on the opposite side of the street. Her pooch was about to be elevated to near royal status. Lance hopped up and down to let his one-man audience know he was excited.

"What?" the doorman asked again, getting annoyed.

"That's a Walker Terrier!"

"A Walker Terrier?"

"I never thought I'd see a Walker Terrier in New York City!"

"What's a Walker Terrier?"

"A Walker Terrier is a very special dog. Let me tell you about it. When the English first established a prison colony in Australia ..."

Plain Jane and her mutt waddled along, and Lance embroidered an elaborate history of the rare and valuable "Walker Terrier" breed.

Minutes passed like years as Lance fed the gullible doorman more and more baloney about the mythical canine.

Lance was still making up lies about the Walker Terrier when the good doctor emerged from the elevator.

"... and so, to this very day, in New South Wales, tickets to the annual Walker Terrier Trials are the most sought-after prizes offered by radio station quiz shows, and ..." Lance paused to acknowledge his client. "Hi, Doc. Everything okay?"

"Everything is just fine."

The Doc and Lance walked away from a very confused doorman.

Outside, as they rounded the corner, Lance asked, "You throw a net over Sean?"

"He's going to be all right now, thanks to you. How much can I pay you for this miracle?"

"Nothing, but I'll keep charging my long distance calls to your calling card."

"That's hardly enough."

"The look on your face right now counts for a lot."

"I do feel greatly relieved. In fact, I think I'm going to walk back to my office. Want to walk with me?"

"Sure. Let me make a call first."

Lance dialed his own number and it rang several times before Janet answered.

The way she answered was even more alarming than her not answering before. "Yaah." Sounded like she was holding her nose.

"Hey, Baby, what's happening?"

"Today is definitely the twenty-seventh! ... Tonight ees pot rroast. Be zair!"

"That it?"

"All for now. Oh, you zee your old friend's son?"

"Not yet."

"He vant zee you reeal bat."

"'kay."

Lance hung up, confused and concerned.

When Lance joined the happy head-shrinker, he noticed Lance looked crestfallen. "You alright?"

"I don't know."

"Walk with me. Maybe we can talk it out."

"I can't walk with you right now. I've got to see a lawyer who'll need your services if I don't get there right away."

"I understand."

Lance wondered precisely what the doctor understood as he hailed a cab.

CHAPTER TWENTY-FIVE

The Big Payoff

• • •

Hysterical or not, Norman Barkley told his British receptionist to ask Lance to wait. Lance thumbed through a magazine, upside down, and barely noticed a well-dressed gentleman check in with Her Majesty. "Matt Cohen for Norm Barkley."

"Is he expecting you, sir?"

"Yes, I called."

"Alright. If you'll just have a seat, I'll tell him you're here."

In a three-piece suit, carrying an expensive briefcase, and sporting buffed nails, Mr. Cohen looked more at home in young Barkley's office suite than Lance. He glanced around and selected a chair at the opposite end of the reception area from where Lance sat. Maybe it was the upside-down magazine which caused him to keep his distance.

The receptionist received a brief call, hung up, and pointed to Lance. "He'll see you now, sir."

Dreading this meeting made Lance's tired body feel at least twice its normal weight. Surely, Norman Barkley summoned him in order to tell him about the crushing humiliation suffered for having relied on him in the first place. The urgency of the call was no doubt because he wanted to share his shame while it was still fresh in his heart.

But life is full of surprises.

The client, for whom Lance had done so little, sat leaning back in his chair with his feet on his desk and a big stogie clenched between his grinning teeth. He looked like Teddy Roosevelt, just back from his charge up San Juan Hill, and posing for a Cuban cigar ad. He pulled the log of tobacco out of his mouth and greeted Lance enthusiastically.

"I'm only sorry you weren't here to enjoy the show!"

"Me too." Lance eased himself down in a chair, wondering what the hell Barkley was talking about.

Pointing with the wet butt of his cigar, Barkley said, "The great man himself, Mr. Daniel Tyler, sat right where you're sitting now." Barkley took a puff, and then pointed again. "Brown stood up over there, and, in that deep stentorian tone of his, demanded, 'Why are we here?'"

Punctuating with jabs of his cigar and mimicking facial expressions, Barkley recreated the scene.

"I simply said, 'Drake.' They both blanched. Tyler gasped out loud. Brown cleared his throat, like thunder, and asked, 'How much?'"

Barkley leaned back again, laughed out loud, and squirmed with delight.

Joy is so rare in the legal profession that it must be fully savored whenever possible.

Barkley said, "I know now what they mean by smelling blood!"

"How much blood did you take?"

"They agreed to pay an undisclosed four million to Drysdale, a publicized four million more to his favorite charities, and public apologies printed in every newspaper which carried the false story, even if Tyler has to pay to print it!"

"Good show!" said Lance. Barkley's glee was infectious.

"How much blood would you like?" asked Barkley.

"I'll leave that to you."

His client looked pensive. "Considering the money Mr. Drysdale paid to others, without results, he was more than happy to pay this firm a flat fee of one million dollars!"

"That's a nice round figure."

"A nice round figure indeed, for just a few days' work. Since you gave me the silver bullet with which I killed the monster, how does two hundred thousand dollars sound? Would that be fair?"

"More than fair."

I have never been paid so much for having done so little.

Lance said, "I'd be happy with half of that in undisclosed cash."

Barkley flinched, and his tone changed completely. He looked suspicious.

"This firm does not deal cash under the table."

"Well, I don't really use much cash, but perhaps we could barter ---"

"Mr. Walker, I don't know what sort of arrangement you had with my father, but I don't play games, particularly in view of with whom I'll be talking next. If two hundred thousand is fair, I'll write you a check. And you can expect your copy of the IRS form 1099 at the end of the year."

"I'm not a tax evader, Mr. Barkley. You can just send my check directly to the Internal Revenue Service."

"Oh. So you do have tax liens to satisfy."

"I do not! I told you at the outset, I don't break laws, not even tax laws."

"But you owe taxes."

"No, I don't. That two hundred thou' will be my estimated tax payments."

"Two hundred thousand estimated income tax? You make a lot of money for a gumshoe."

"A lot of it is in cash or in kind, but I file a more accurate tax return than most people."

"Why then would you offer to barter?"

"The IRS has harassed me for years because I won't keep records, so I'm particularly careful to pay taxes."

"No books or records?"

"No. I have to protect the identities of my clients. You're an exception. Most of my clients want anonymity."

"How do you keep track of your tax liability?"

"In my head."

Surprisingly, Barkley didn't look surprised. He nodded knowingly and summarized what Lance had said. "So even though you pay all your taxes in a timely fashion, the IRS is harassing you for the identities of your clients?"

"That's correct."

"No, it's not, or it shouldn't be. If you don't mind repeating what you've just told me, my best friend, Matt Cohen, is waiting outside. I don't really know why he's here, but he just happens to be the Regional Director of the IRS, and I think he'd be shocked to hear how you're being treated."

The Regional Director of the IRS! What an opportunity. In the past, I couldn't even get a human being on the telephone at the Internal Revenue Service, let alone speak with the top man, himself. Come on Lance, don't screw this up.

Lance followed Barkley to the door. Barkley opened it and summoned his pal from the waiting room. "Matt."

Cohen stood up, walked to the door, and handed Barkley a legal looking document. "I hate to do this, Norm, but I've got to serve you with a summons. I figured you'd rather get it from me."

Barkley looked surprised. "Am I a target?"

"No," the IRS boss said. "It's just for information you may have about a guy your dad once represented, briefly."

Barkley didn't look at the document, very un-lawyer-like.

"Okay," said Barkley, "no problem. Let me introduce you to a guy who *is* a target of your agency. Mr. Walker, this is my oldest and best friend, Matt Cohen."

"Walker!" Matt Cohen jumped back a step. "Lance Walker?"

"Hi," said Lance with a sheepish grin. He tried to look warm and fuzzy.

Cohen turned to Barkley. "You represent Mr. Walker, Norm?"

"Does he need representation?"

"Look at the summons," said Cohen.

Barkley looked.

Lance guessed his name was on it.

"I will represent Mr. Walker, if he wants me to, but so far Mr. Walker has been representing me." Barkley looked to Lance for an opinion. "Want me to represent you?"

"Go ahead."

Barkley looked back and forth from Lance to Cohen and back to Lance.

"Can we all step into my office?"

The bad news bearer and Lance followed Barkley back into his sanctum.

Barkley summarized what Lance had told him, and then Cohen interrogated Lance for the better part of an hour. Lance figured this was the most friendly opportunity he would ever get to plead his case with the IRS, so he didn't hold anything back, except, of course, the names of his clients.

After Lance had softened him up, the Regional Administrator confided an interesting story.

"The first time I laid eyes on Mr. Whittaker, he was bandaged up like the walking-wounded. I told him I was sorry Satan's Savages had welcomed him to New York before I did."

Lance wrinkled his brow and pretended his ignorance was pure, so far as Satan's Savages were concerned. Sincerity is the key; once you learn to fake that ---

Cohen went on, "Whittaker's family stayed in Texas because he plans to retire soon, and Texas is where they want to live. He's been eligible to retire for over a year."

"So why did he take the disciplinary transfer to New York?" asked Lance, "He could have retired and stayed right there in Texas."

"He wants his grade back. It would enhance his retirement benefits, considerably. Hell, he could have gone back to Texas to recuperate at home, but he insisted he wasn't as bad off as he looked. He said he was onto a taxpayer with a network of sophisticated people illicitly supporting his personal underground economy."

"That'd be me," said Lance.

"Exactly. When I pointed out that you would still be here when he came back from sick leave, he said, 'That's the trouble with guys in this Region. No one's caught the scent of the chase. Walker has eluded you for over twenty years!'"

Cohen's imitation of Whittaker's Texas accent was uncanny. He continued it, "'I figure if I nail a guy that no other Group Supervisor has laid a glove on, you'll promote me to Branch Chief and I can retire happy.'"

"Did you make a deal with him?" asked Barkley.

"I told him I couldn't promise anything. He said, 'If I can deliver, so can you,' and I didn't tell him 'No.'"

Barkley asked, "So what's the deal now?"

"I can't officially forgive Mr. Walker's course of action, but ..."

CHAPTER TWENTY-SIX

Meanwhile Back At Janet's Office

• • •

The phone rang several times before Janet picked it up, holding her nose. "Yaah."

This time Lance was leaning back in Barkley's big chair with his feet on the big oak desk and a huge, expensive cigar in his mouth.

"Sorry to be a party pooper, but I have a dinner date for pasta tonight, so I'll just have to join you for pot roast some other time."

"I reeeally must zee you," Janet mimicked.

"About the IRS agents serving summonses on all the lawyers and accountants who have ever represented me?"

Barkley and Cohen puffed their own cigars, grinned, and enjoyed Lance's half of the conversation.

Janet must have let go of her nose. Suddenly her voice was normal. "You sure you want to talk about this on the phone?"

"I negotiated a cease-fire with the IRS. They can't quit, officially, but I'm not supposed to hear from them again, so long as I keep paying my taxes."

His puffing buddies nodded in affirmation.

"Am I ever again going to see that bandaged baboon who busted into my office?"

"Whittaker came to your office?"

"He all but broke in. When Cynthia buzzed me to say he was here, he walked right by her. I got my door locked just in time. He kept banging on it while I was shredding your message slips, dropping them all over the floor—scared the hell out of me."

"Did you let him in?"

Janet paused. "Yes."

She was too well-mannered not to answer her door, but she rationalized her response, "I thought he would break it down if I didn't."

"You should have called nine-one-one."

She sighed. "I know that now. It all happened so fast. He pushed me aside, limped in, and handed me a forthwith-summons."

"What did the summons call for?"

"Any information I might have on clients of my baby brother. I told him I didn't have any documents. The shredder was humming; I had left it on! He said, 'The summons doesn't say *documents,* it calls for any *information* you may have on who contacts him.'"

Lance's sister mimicked Whittaker's accent almost as well as Cohen had.

"I told him I'm not a tax lawyer, but there's got to be something dreadfully wrong with this. He said, 'Sign on the door says you're a lawyer. You refusing to comply? You know the repercussions if you don't? You can comply right now or suffer the consequences.' I said I was going to have to look at this summons and give him a call. He baited me, 'You sure that's what you want to do?' He was so menacing! Then your phone started ringing! I couldn't answer it with him standing here. He knew it had to be something to do with you."

"That must have been me calling this afternoon."

"Well, Whittaker really enjoyed watching me squirm. I told him to get out of my office, and he said, 'Don't come whining to me when you get yourself held in contempt ... and get disbarred ... and get jailed ... and get audited ... regularly.' I told him I never whine, and he said, 'See you in court, counselor. You lawyers don't know when not to mess with the IRS. That's why we put more lawyers in jail than any other profession!'

After I pushed him out the door, your phone stopped ringing."

"Like I said," Lance said, "it was only me."

"Oh. Okay. What are we going to do about this rodeo Revenue Officer?"

"In the morning, he's being promoted for piercing my cash-and-carry conspiracy, on the condition that he retires to Texas–*immediately*!"

Cohen and Barkley kept puffing, kept smiling, and kept nodding.

Janet said, "Texas isn't far enough!"

"Where would you like him to go? Never mind, I can guess. I've got to go now, got to see an FBI agent before pasta time."

CHAPTER TWENTY-SEVEN

Bonsignore Means Good Woman, Too

• • •

When Lance phoned her, Special Agent Bonsignore said, "You should never come to my office again. I can't protect your identity as my source of information about Vinnie Manarino if you keep showing up here. Someone who knows you might see you."

Lance said, "That's already happened, but it turned out okay. How about we meet in a coffee shop near the 59th Street Bridge?"

"Can you give me the exact location?"

"Sure."

Ms. Bonsignore got there first.

Lance spotted her as soon as he stepped through the door. It's hard to hide a well-stacked, longhaired blonde with fashion-model looks. Lance glanced around but, unfortunately, didn't see anyone he knew.

I'd love someone I know to see me with this babe.

The meeting didn't last long. She came right to the point and they shook on it.

Just like every other guy in the place, Lance watched her walk away.

Sixty seconds later, without even checking for counter-surveillance, Lance glided out after her.

She boarded the cable car to Roosevelt Island. Lance wondered if she lived over there, and if someday he might be her overnight guest.

CHAPTER TWENTY-EIGHT

No Good Deed Goes Unpunished

• • •

Lance had to hurry to get to the library before it closed. A buck-and-a-half bus fare reduced his taxable income to $218,685.44, but the transfer for the cross-town bus was free.

His rubber heels *thunked* loudly on the bare floor in the cavernous Research Room. His Research Librarian was all alone, doing paperwork.

"Excuse me, ma'am."

She lifted her petite face and shined those wonderful blue-gray eyes on him.

"Yes, sir."

"I couldn't help but overhear yesterday when you were talking about how much your son likes the New York Yankees."

"Yes?" She looked suspicious.

"Well, I don't."

"So?" She shot little looks from the corners of her eyes.

She's probably seeking help or planning an escape route.

"So this morning a friend gave me two season tickets to the Yankees games."

Lance handed her Mr. Lee's tickets.

"I have no use for them. I'd like you to take your son to the games."

She turned the tickets over and over in her hand.

Looking for attached strings, I suppose.

"Why me?" she asked.

"'Cause I heard how much your son is a New York Yankees fan."

"I can't afford these."

She tried to give them back.

Lance held up his open palms.

"No charge."

Her mouth was a frozen *O* when Lance turned to walk away.

"Sir!"

Lance stopped and turned back.

"Yes, ma'am."

"You're serious."

"Yes, ma'am."

"I don't even know your name."

"Walker. Lance Walker."

"Well ..." Tears welled up in her blue-gray eyes. "I'm Monica Perez ... my son, Travis, ---"

Lance tried to cut her suffering short. "—will just love the Yankees games."

"I don't know how to thank you."

"Just take Travis to the ball games."

New Yorkers can withstand anything but kindness. Lance felt rotten that he made her cry. He turned away again.

"Mr. Walker."

She's not through making me feel bad.

Lance turned to face her once more.

"Ms. Perez?"

She looked all around, then said, "My extension here is 3606. If you ever need anything, just ask for me." She smiled through her tears.

Lance smiled, too.

"Okay. I may just do that."

A few steps later she tried to stop him, again.

"Don't you want to write it down?"

Lance didn't stop walking.

"Nah, I got it."

His soft shoes softly thumped away through the smell of old books.

The long walk up Broadway did Lance good.

CHAPTER TWENTY-NINE

At Ease

• • •

An hour from the library, Lance had a warm woman pressed against either side of him, and the aroma of a marvelous marinara sauce filling his nostrils. He was seated between Helen Karris and Sofia O'Shea at Helen's dining table eating Sofia's pasta.

Lance said, "You were right, Helen, Sofia is a great cook."

"I told you."

Sofia said, "It's just pasta."

Helen rose. "It's time for my news now. I'll leave you two alone."

Sofia and Lance rolled their eyes at one another, uncomfortably.

Lance stood up and told Helen, "We'll get the dishes."

"Good. I'll go to bed after the news. I'm glad you can stay over."

That remark made Sofia and Lance feel even *more* uncomfortable.

When Helen was out of sight, Lance told Sofia, "Don't worry. I'm sleeping on the couch, but I am looking forward to fixing you breakfast in the morning."

"I'd like that," said Sofia as she rose to her feet.

"The FBI agreed to our deal. The very clever agent figured out that Marty's retirement payments are wired to Wanda's account, so if they were divorced that constitutes *Fraud by Wire*, a law the FBI investigates. They will check around for the divorce if we keep giving them information about Vinnie Manarino. When they finish checking Southern California, we'll need to provide some more stuff."

"You should make a deal for yourself—with the IRS."

"I did. Now I want you to remember the names of the people Vinnie pays."

"Close my eyes, right?" She closed her eyes.

"Yeah."

What a beautiful face she has.

"Take deep slow breaths, right?"

Nice boobs, too.

With her eyes closed, Sofia stepped forward, slipped her arms over his shoulders and pressed her soft body against his chest. Lance closed his eyes.

What an exquisite moment, his dream coming true—her fluffy hair tickling his face, her warm breath on his neck, her panting in his ear—he moaned with pleasure without opening his eyes.

Quivering with excitement, eager for his touch, she stuck her hot, wet tongue in his ear and jolted him wide awake.

He grabbed her abundant hair with both hands and gently pushed her back.

But this time it wasn't Ralph's Afghan hound, Ginger. Lance was looking into the eyes of a gorgeous Italian-American who was licking her lips and watching him fidget, a smile on those lips.

"I forgot where I was," said Lance.

"*You* forgot?"

"Yeah, I know, I'm the guy who never forgets anything."

Lance wrapped his arms around her and lifted her easily off the floor, her soft body radiating heat.

"What a deal," said Sofia.

Those tender lips were even warmer than her body. It was a very long kiss.

The End

If you have enjoyed ***Forewarned***, you might like to read the author's novel: ***A Year In Fear***, which is written in a similar style. It is the story of a petite, young female police detective in a small town, struggling with quirky cases, throughout her rookie year.

ABOUT THE AUTHOR

Harry Gossett's investigative experience covers a vast variety of cases, and locations, and spans decades, including eight years in New York City, the setting for *Forewarned*.

—

"Harry Gossett brings street smarts and savvy humor to fiction, with the kind of insightful, authentic voice that's a joy to find. Read him, you won't regret it."
>James Grady, author of
>**LAST DAYS OF THE CONDOR**

Made in the USA
Lexington, KY
20 January 2015